IF I HAD A
MILLION
DOLLARS

TIMOTHY P. MUNKEBY'S

IF I HAD A
MILLION
DOLLARS

HOW TO ACHIEVE FINANCIAL INDEPENDENCE
Before your parents do!

BEAVER'S
POND
PRESS

ISBN 10: 1-59298-277-8
ISBN 13: 978-1-59298-277-6

Library of Congress Catalog Number: 2009923308

Printed in the United States of America

First Printing: 2009

13 12 11 10 09   5 4 3 2 1

Cover and interior design by James Monroe Design, LLC.

BEAVER'S
POND
PRESS

Beaver's Pond Press, Inc.
7104 Ohms Lane, Suite 101
Edina, MN 55439–2129
(952) 829-8818
www.BeaversPondPress.com

To order, visit www.BookHouseFulfillment.com
or call 1-800-901-3480. Reseller discounts available.

*To the students and all of my clients who have made my two careers so enjoyable...
and what a gas to now, in my Heydays, culminate in the two.*

*I would also like to acknowledge Margie Johnson, of Tower, Minnesota,
and my daughter, Alexandra, for their help with this book,
and especially my daughter-in-law, Lisa Munkeby, who can do anything.*

CONTENTS

PREFACE

If you're entering or have just entered the work force, you need to read this book...so you, at least, will *know* what you have to do to become financially independent. You'll be busting your butt to make a buck. What you do with that buck, now, will determine how happy your life is, later.

"You don't need a weatherman to know which way the wind blows."[†]

—*Bob Dylan*—

1938

"One of the lasting changes made by the Depression is that it has shown people that they cannot live beyond their earnings."

—Mary Hinsman Able,
Journal of Home Economics, January 1938—

2008

"Americans are progress junkies: we expect tomorrow to be better off than today. But, we may be on the cusp of an era that frustrates this expectation—a state of 'affluent deprivation.' The personal savings rate dropped from 11% in 1982 to about zero by 2005."

—Robert Samuelson, "A Darker Future for Us,"
Newsweek 10-10-08—

2038

Americans haven't learned. They didn't change. If you don't want a darker future for yourself, you must change things, now.

CHAPTER 1

YOUR WAY

Revolution

They say "change is pain," but sometimes the pain of not changing is more painful than changing. When this happens with the masses or an entire generation, we have the roots of a revolution.

We had a revolution in America. I'm speaking not of the minor revolutions like the Industrial Revolution, but the big honcho, the American Revolution, that supposedly freed us to be better off than our mothers and fathers.

This is the American right we believed we had earned: to be better off than the generation before us. But the baby boomers have, unwittingly, severely challenged that right. They caught a disease, "affluenza," that's created a financial crisis in this country that will burden every generation to follow.

That's you, by the by.

Dave Barry's right. After WWII the government encouraged Americans to spend, spend, spend to avoid another depression or a severe recession. Save and sacrifice during the war, then seek prosperity by buying everything in sight after the war. So we can't put all the blame on the boomers, but they sure as hell ran with this new New Deal.

Because of this, 80% of them will be running long past the age when they wanted to slow down. If you follow their path, you'll end up right where they are. And where are they? Let's take a look at a few headlines I've collected the last few years:

• • •

Boomers Can't Retire...
Most Will Have to Work Late in Life

• • •

80% of People Polled Believe
They Will Run Out of Money in
Their Lifetime

• • •

The Average Baby Boomer
Has Saved Less Than $80,000
for Retirement

• • •

> *"Hey! The world wasn't exactly perfect when we got here."*
> —Dave Barry,
> Baby Boomer, from *Dave Turns 50*—

Workers Between the Ages of 25 and
45 Have, On Average, Less Than $10,000
Saved for Retirement

• • •

Savings Rate at a Negative

• • •

We Have a Pension/Retirement Crisis
That May Be the Equal of No Other
American Crisis

• • •

Americans Found Illiterate in Saving,
Investing

• • •

Credit Card Debt Reaching
All-Time Highs

• • •

Home Foreclosures Hitting
All-Time Highs

• • •

The Average College Student Graduates with
Nearly $10,000 in Credit Card Debt and
$20,000 in Student Loans

• • •

Almost 50% of All College Graduates
Move Back In with Parents
After They Graduate

• • •

• • •

**Keeping Your Kids Afloat:
As the Cost of Living Soars, More Young
Adults are Turning to Their Parents for
Financial Help. Sometimes the Best Help of All
is Saying 'No.'**

• • •

**Workers Near Retirement Have Saving Advice
for Younger People: Start Early and Don't Stop,
or Your Dreams May Blow Away**

• • •

"Staging a mini-consumer revolt is easy.
Pay attention to where every single one of
your hard-earned dollars is going. After
all, only you know exactly what kind of
bullshit you had to do in order to earn
them in the first place."[†]

–Lydia Lunch, Artist–

How did we get in this mess? Professor David Tucker in his book, *The Decline of Thrift in America: Shift from Saving to Spending*, blames it on "now-now-ism,"…"self-indulgent theft from the future." [Your future!]

"Americans and their government continue to live beyond their means…thrift is essential for survival…the abandonment of thrift is largely responsible for our current economic position…until actual economic catastrophe strikes."

In the mid-seventies we experienced an energy crisis. It was thought that catastrophe would change behavior: consume less, buy small gas-efficient cars, save more, and accumulate less debt.

When Professor Tucker's book came out in 1991, the government had just **bailed out** thousands of banks and saving and loans.

So Americans had not perserveded in changing their habits. They spent us into the 2000 bubble that burst and we all gasped: Is this the end? We have to consume less; reduce our debt, save more…But big, honking gas-guzzling SUVs became the top sellers, and the sales on expensive luxury cars increased dramatically throughout the recession during the first few years of this millennium until:

2007 and 2008!! Another Great Depression?! One headline read, "The End of Wall Street!!" Bailouts, bankruptcies, foreclosures. Is this the catastrophe that will finally spawn a revolution? Americans haven't seen the light…they haven't changed their destructive, consuming behavior. You've got to be the one to change things…yes you. You need to lead the way…or each catastrophe will get worse—affecting your generation more than any other.

Sorry for being so glum and laying it on you, but don't blame me. I'm in the 20% for whom you won't have to pay nursing home costs. True, it's most of my generation passing this mess on to you. But it's quite remarkable that you can change things… change the world as a matter of fact, with each of you staging your own personal revolution, so you won't be in the 80% that run out of money.

> "To live is the rarest thing in the world. Most people exist, that is all."[†]
>
> —Oscar Wilde—

Retirement Redefined

I'm sorry that you're inheriting such a mess. Rather than follow in the boomers' footsteps, who paid everyone but themselves, working late into their lives at a job they hate because they can't afford to retire, realize you do have a choice.

Knowing what you need to do—education—is the first step. Yet, even after classes on financial literacy, high school and college students have miserably failed national financial literacy tests. So, understandably, do their parents. This is because facts and figures—information alone—cannot change lifelong bad habits. Change requires a revolution: a complete reversal of habits…to realize your dreams or goals, you must start to prepare…*now.*

> *Heydays:*
> *the time of greatest health,*
> *vigor, beauty, prosperity;*
> *the prime of your life.*
>
> —Daniel Webster—

I hope to be able to motivate you to form good habits so that you can become free…independent, working at what you want for as long as you want, rather than working at something you don't enjoy well into your Heydays.

Your choice is to start now to work toward your dream of how you would like to live your life. Start a revolution, your own *personal* revolution. All you have to do is change how you look at money…and your life. Your reward for participating in this revolution (which is inevitable and necessary) is freedom:

To be doing with your life what you really want to be doing, as early as possible, and for as long as you want to.

This is the new "retirement." Doing what you love instead of drudging away at something you're tired of doing until you're 60 or 65 or, as with 80% of the boomers, into your 70s or 80s.

The new retirement: doing what you want to be doing as soon as possible; and doing it as often as you like and for as long as you want to.

The 80/20 Rule

So far, I've mentioned 80% several times. There's an 80/20 rule that's remarkably accurate: 20% of people pay 80% of the taxes; 20% of people have 80% of the children; 20% of athletes make 80% of the money; 20% of fishermen catch 80% of the fish.

By this rule, 20% of you will reach financial independence, and 80% of you will not. I know you're young and "retirement" seems so far off, so I figure only 20% of you will listen and realize you have to start your revolution, *now*. The sooner you change, the more likely you will succeed. And that's the way it needs to be. The 20% of you who will be independent, doing what *you* want to be doing early in your lives, need the other 80% to continue to spend, consume, and drive the economy. History has proven it's the poor who are the spenders. The successful 20% have paid themselves, which is why they have money.

If you want to make sure you end up in the 20%, enjoying the hell out of your life, keep reading. Consider these suggestions, forging your own path to financial freedom…and a contented life. You'll awake to the sun in your Heydays, while the other 80% will drag themselves out of bed in the dark to the blare of an alarm.

> "The human mind treats a new idea the way a body treats a strange protein; it rejects it."[‡]
>
> – P.D. Medawar, Biologist –

Maslow's Flight Plan

I don't know if you've come across "Maslow's Hierarchy" in your school days, but I like what it suggests to us about our lives: we start with basic needs, then build toward higher rewards.

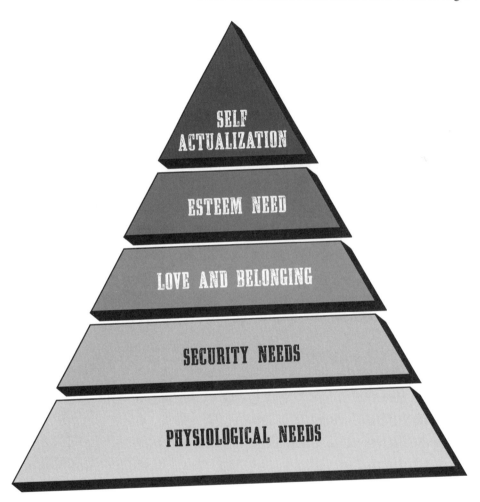

- Self-Actualization (realize all inner potential)
- Esteem Need (to be unique, to have self-respect)
- Love and Belonging (appreciation, friendship)
- Security Needs (family and society)
- Physiological Needs (food and shelter)

If you become stuck on paying the bills, living paycheck to paycheck, you're stranded on the bottom of Maslow's Hierarchy and your life will not be as fulfilling as you'd like. You should be on a life-long flight up that hierarchy to self-actualization, not tethered to self-subsistence.

So, I want to persuade you to do what you need to move gracefully up Maslow's flight plan…and to start *now*. Once you get trapped in consumerism, spending beyond your means, it's possible, but difficult, to get out. Realize that owing more than you own, or spending more than you make, is not sustainable. If you are an average person, you saw between 20,000 and 40,000 television commercials each year, according to the Center for a New American Dream. And that doesn't include the radio or the internet, which has created a whole new paradigm of buying junkies and shopping addicts. You're in a culture that promotes living beyond your means. PBS produces a special entitled, *"Affluenza: The All-consuming Epidemic."* They defined affluenza as: *"…a painful, contagious, socially transmitted condition of over-load, debt, anxiety, and waste resulting from the dogged pursuit of more."*

Sound like fun? Are you in the 80% susceptible to affluenza? Are you going to swim with the stream, or against it?

> "Pleasures go stale, but happiness is always fresh and fulfilling. The most important ingredient in happiness is self-esteem: the knowledge that it is good to be who you are."[†]
>
> – Roger Scruton, Philsopher –

> "… death is not the most grievous of your losses. Far worse is to live too long, clinging to a life that has lost its enchantment."[†]
>
> –John Shirley, Writer–

"There are things in life money can't buy, for everything else there's Master Card"…this makes buying seem so fun…so innocent. Guess you can "charge" stupidity? Sorry if I'm offending anyone…but, really, don't you agree? Robert D. Manning, author of *Credit Card Nation: The Consequences of America's Addiction to Credit,* has updated the debt figures that were in my earlier headlines: college graduates will owe closer to $30,000 in student loans and $15,000 in credit card debt. Since the average salary of the college graduate is $22,000, bankruptcy is the likely outcome. What a great way to start a career?! If you're in this predicament, go ahead and move back home. But, go to work, pay off your loans ASAP, *and* save—pay yourself—as well. Oh, and be nice to, respectful of, and gracious to your parents.

So are you strong enough to avoid consumer addiction?

Obsequious (dead fish) or revolutionary? Your choice. Your way.

> *"Only dead fish swim with the stream."*[†]
>
> – Unknown –

> Obsequious is a good word. In case you don't know it: "Excessively willing to serve or obey; overly submissive."
>
> – Daniel Webster –

> "At least once a day stand before a mirror and repeat after me: 'I'm not a Buick, I'm a Buddha!'
>
> At least once a week, renew a solemn vow to limit consumption.
>
> At least once a month, remind yourself that your purpose on earth is to enlargen your soul, light up your brain, and liberate your spirit.
>
> At least once a year, go out and sleep where the bears sleep.
>
> Thus, having gotten mind and body in orderyou are free to climbaboard that strange torpedo and ride it to wherever it's going."
>
> – Tom Robbins –

Questions

1. Do you, at this point in your life, feel you may not be better off, financially, than your parents when you reach their age? Why?

_____

_____

_____

_____

_____

_____

_____

2. A _Time_ magazine article, "America's Health Check-up," 12/1/08, stated: "…experts fear that this generation of American kids may be the first ever to have a shorter life span than their parents do." It proposed this is due to lack of exercise, poor eating habits, and stress. Why or why don't you believe this? How does this affect you and how you live your life?

_____

_____

_____

_____

_____

_____

_____

3. Do you feel that in your life you have had any contact with the issues raised in the headlines? If so, which ones, and how will you avoid being a headline? If not, why and what will you do to ensure you're not a headline?

_____

_____

_____

_____

_____

_____

_____

4. Comment on how you think "retirement" should be defined;

_____

_____

_____

_____

5. Do you think you'll be in the 20% awakening to the sun or the 80% to the blare of an alarm? Why? Think it's a bunch of bull or a real-life planning concern?

_____

_____

_____

_____

_____

_____

6. If you had to design, at this point in your life, how you'd reach your "inner potential" in your Heydays, what would it be you'd be doing with your life? To help you ponder may I suggest you consider: if you had all the money in the world right now, what would you do with your life? Don't be cute and say "nothing." Nothing gets boring real quick.

_____

_____

_____

_____

_____

_____

_____

_____

7. Are you afflicted with "affluenza?" Why or why not? What are you going to do, if anything, about it?

_____

_____

_____

_____

_____

_____

_____

_____

_____

8. Do you currently have credit card debt? What do you plan to do about it whether you do or don't?

_____

_____

_____

_____

_____

_____

9. Do you think we need a revolution? Why or why not?

_____

_____

_____

_____

_____

_____

THE PREMISE

Buying Freedom

You've been taught all your life how to make money, but not what to do once you have some.

So if you had a million dollars, what would you do with it? A BMW Roadster might be cool. Buy your boyfriend a fishing boat? Your girlfriend a windjammer cruise with Johnny Depp? (Maybe not.) Your mom a shopping trip to New York… Tiffany's? Your dad a Craftsman table saw? For your grandmother a trip to Nice would be nice. A horse with a rhinestone

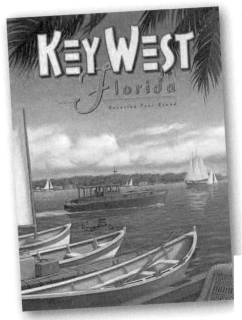

bridle? A little place in Key West? A cabin up north on a lake? Man, there's a lot of stuff that would be nice to have if you had a million dollars. What would you buy if you had a million dollars?

May I suggest, as I mentioned earlier, that you buy freedom. Freedom? You're already free, you say? I don't know: as a child you did what your parents wanted. As a student you did what your teachers wanted. And when you get that first job, you will do what your boss wants. And don't forget today's advertising gurus.

They have you figured out. They know what makes you tick. You even do what they want. They want you to
want, **WANT, *WANT!!***
 Spend! **SPEND! *SPEND!!***

Freedom? I don't know. The older you get the less freedom you have…giving up independence…not doing what *you* want but what *they* want.

When do I get to do what I want? How can a million dollars buy freedom? A million dollars, invested appropriately, could give you an income of $50,000 a year, adjusted each year for inflation, for the rest of your life. Imagine: if you had $50,000 of income each year and lived within those means, you wouldn't have to kowtow to a boss. You could pick your life's passion without worrying, "How much will I make?" Your only concern will be: "Is this what I want to be doing?" Webster defines independent as:

• • •

"self-reliant, uncontrolled, un-coerced, unconstrained…free, autonomous."
…in other words, in control of your own life.

"solvent well-to-do
in easy circumstances."
…in other words, not in heavy debt.

• • •

Yeah, fine. Sounds nice…but, "I don't have a million dollars," you say. While you may not now, you can have this in your future. Let's say the average lifetime salary, today, is $75,000. That means, if you are only average, you'll make over 2.5 million dollars in your lifetime. If you kept only 10% of that and invested it in the S&P 500 (index of the largest 500 companies in the U.S.) and the average annual return was the same as it's been the last 100

$75,000/yr. = $2,500,000

Save 10% = $1,000,000
Save 20% = $2,000,000

years, you would have a million dollars by the time you are 50 (average savings of $541/month). You'd have $2 million if you kept 20%. You could take all your old high school friends to Aruba for spring break. You could paint or draw, write, make folk furniture, travel, kayak white water, backpack the Rockies, sail…you could do what you want, put the kids through school and everything…and still do what you want and enjoy your life, regardless of what "The Man" says.

Many of the baby boomers pretty much sold their souls. They didn't pay themselves for their work. They got trapped, fell prey to consumerism, bought stuff, and paid everybody else. You're going to have to be stronger and revolt. You're going to have to pay yourself *first*. The sooner you start investing a minimum of 10% of what you make, the better. The average boomer had well over a million dollars and spent it. We currently have, according to government statistics, a "negative" savings rate, as one of the headlines at the beginning stated. Unfortunately Generations X and Y ahead of you are following in the boomers' footsteps, and may be forced to work at something they didn't choose long past when they wanted to slow down or retire…unless they change and adapt.

> "Now, some of you may encounter the devil's bargain: any old soul is worth savingbut not every soul is worth buying. They try the easy ones first—you know, the ones who love money—all the money there is— but who wants to be the richest guy in the cemetery? So piss off Satan, and don't take me for dumber than I look."[†]
>
> – Wm S. Burroughs –

10% starting with your 1st paycheck = $ 1 million by age 50.

How did boomers get into this mess? A life of poor role models, and a life of living beyond their means, with too much debt—credit cards being the primary culprit—and thus the inability to save or to pay themselves. Too many boomers have very little set aside for their "Heydays," and the home that has appreciated nicely is financed to the hilt…financed to buy scat…

> "*Scat: Animal droppings. In other words sh*t.*"[‡]
>
> – Daniel Webster –

stuff that is temporary, temporal, and eventually worthless.

I hope to tempt you to: 1) Stay out of "bad" debt by 2) living within your means and 3) paying yourself at least 10% of what you make, starting with your first paycheck. Pay yourself first and regularly, not at the end of the month with what money you have left or, like the generations before you, you'll have nothing left to save.

> *"Status Quo. Latin for 'the mess we're in."*[‡]
>
> – Jeve Moorman –

Not Just About Money

So, don't get me wrong. This isn't really just about money. Money is nowhere near the most important thing in life. While it's certainly important, and may indeed make "the world go 'round," or at least help you go 'round the world, it's not worth going 'round at all without family, friends, and good health. In my world, balance in life has always been more important than earning a lot of money. A career that I enjoy and am passionate about is more fulfilling than one that just paid a good salary. They say, "You can't buy love," but many of you and your parents have been raised to think you can charge it.

"Financial literacy is not something you're born with," says Robert Duvall, Chief Executive of the National Council of Economic Education. Good personal finance habits are "learned

> "My generation has passed on a diminished legacy on earth with terrible dangers and debts. Think about what you actually need for a good life, not what friends or ads have taught you what you want. You are not what you own. Do not measure yourself or others by the yardstick of money. Do what is possible within the reach of your voice and hands; trust that others elsewhere are doing their part."[†]
>
> – Scott Russell Sanders –

"I'd advise young people to visit morgues and see as many bodies as they can. There's no doubt in my mind that once you begin to have a clear sense that you're going to die, you really begin to live—and that's all there really is, because the meaning of life is in the living of it."

– Spalding Gray

On Beautiful Lake Vermilion

BIRCH POINT INN

On Birch Point

TOWER, MINNESOTA

AAA

Aerial View of Birch Point Inn and Boat Harbor.

..*Summer Fun!*
in family portions

- WATER SKIING
- BASKETBALL COURT
- VOLLEYBALL COURT
- HIGH WATER SLIDE
- SHUFFLEBOARD
- HORSESHOES
- RAFT AND DIVING BOARD
- AND FISHING

behavior." So, I am attempting to "*learn*" you. I am not presuming to *tell* you what you should do with your money...or anything else for that matter. I learned that in parenting, teaching, coaching, and financial planning, if people look up to you, they model their behavior after you. I also learned in my careers not to tell people what to do, but to ask questions to help them arrive at what they want to do. So...do you want to be stressed, fight with your spouse over money (the number-one cause of divorce is money problems) and work 60 hours a week at a job you hate until you're 120?

People simply do not like to be told what to do. I know I don't. So I'm going to show you what worked for me... and you do what you like. But, hopefully, after hearing or reading this at least you know you have a choice. If you were raised as if you could buy love, or anything else you wanted, with plastic, let this be a refreshing slap in the face. Wake up and realize that plastic, like money, is worthless in and of itself...but it sure can get you into a heap of trouble if you're stupid...sorry: "financially illiterate."

This is a brochure for the resort my parents first took me to when I was three years old. The idea of a crystal clear lake with a sand beach and wilderness shoreline to explore stayed with me all my life. I knew that someday, that's what I wanted. That was my dream. Whenever I tucked away some savings, in the back of my mind... was Lake Vermilion in northern Minnesota by the Boundary Waters. I knew that one day, after school days and work days, that in my Heydays, that's where I wanted to "make hay."

*To realize a dream later
you must defer income now.*

If you already know what your dream is, you're fortunate because you'll have the motivation to do now what I'm attempting to show you. Your dream right now might be to get a good job, earn a lot of money, be successful in a career… but you'll realize, eventually, a job, a career, is a means to an end…an end, that if you "buy" independence, should be happy. You'll eventually realize your lifelong dream for your Heydays and have the resources and time to live it. I started "buying" independence when I was nine years old. In the last chapter, I'll show you how this got me to where I am today in my Heydays, living my dream, and how I did it earlier than most.

After "Work Days," you enter the final stage of your life… your "Heydays." This is when *you*, not someone else, should be in control of your life. Have you ever sat through a boring class or had a job where you watched the clock…the minutes slowly ticking away until you were free? If you don't want to be doing this your entire life, you need to start planning now.

My Three Stages

Since it's my book, I am (as you may have noticed) dividing our lives into three stages: School Days, Work Days, and Heydays. Our priorities change and evolve through these stages. In our early School Days our priorities are family, friends and play—which, if active, is probably synonymous with health at this stage. The school variable depends to a great extent on the importance our parents place on it for us. A plan for the future and a career is not important yet.

As we get older, school may become our top priority: Am I going to go to college? A tech school? Where? Will I be accepted? You'll add: "What should I major in?" to your list of priorities. Hopefully education is a high priority for you because it is such an expensive commodity. You may need loans to help with the cost, but hopefully you've kept, or will keep, these to a minimum because it's hard to get out from under them when you graduate.

> *"It's easier to stay out than get out."*[‡]
>
> – Mark Twain –

When we enter our "Work Days," we tend to put a higher priority on our job or career, letting our other priorities suffer...but try to maintain balance: family, friends, and health. A plan for the future also suddenly looms as a priority when we realize we don't want to work forever and would like to enter our Heydays while we can still make hay. Our work, hopefully, has been enjoyable and even a passion, but it may also have become more of a means to an end...an end to our Work Days. In your Heydays, unfortunately (or fortunately), your financial situation may determine how active you are, how much leisure time you have, and the condition of your health. Financially sound people are more active, less stressed, and thus are generally in better health...and live longer. Even if you haven't figured out your retirement dream yet, just living long ain't a bad goal, for now. But wouldn't it be a boot in the butt to discover what your dream is, but you have defered working toward it, and so when you finally realize just what it is that you want to do with your life, you're not financially prepared—you're "rotten meat?"

• • •

A Dream Deferred
by Langston Hughes

What happens to a dream deferred?
Does it dry up
like a raisin in the sun?
Or fester like a sore –
And then run?
Does it stink like rotten meat?
Or crust and sugar over –
Like a syrupy sweet?

Maybe it just sags
Like a heavy load.

Or does it just explode?

• • •

Langston Hughes in his poem "A Dream Deferred" showed us the hopelessness of a dream unattained. Don't think you can defer what you need to do, now, or your dreams may blow away and be deferred forever.

The purpose for your Work Days is two-fold. The first goal is to support yourself by living within your means. To do this, you must have a **ZERO BALANCE** on your credit card debt each month. I have nothing against credit cards; I use them all the time. But you must pay them off every month, period. The second goal is to provide you and your family with funds to create income for living the way you want in your Heydays. To do this you have to **PAY YOURSELF**

> "What if it were possible to be a little more awake, a little more conscious, so that you can do what you really want to do – so that you can find out what that is – and so that you're not just blundering along. How many times do you hear people who go into a career, put twenty-five years into it and then say, 'It seemed like a good idea at the time.'"
>
> – John Shirley –

FIRST every month, or every paycheck. Nobody else is going to do this for you. Even if you have a government or union job with a pension, you'll still need to pay yourself something regularly. A rule of thumb is that 10% of what you make, minimum, goes to a "retirement fund." Do not, I repeat do *not*, think you can retire on social security.

People who are truly independent by what we might call "early retirement age" will save closer to 15 to 25% of what they earned. Again, living within your means…means starting to pay yourself *immediately* at that first job, and living on the rest. It does not matter how much you earn. Did you register that? I work with people who made modest incomes, kept and invested 10-20% of what they made, and are financially independent at a relatively early age. Remember: the earlier you start saving, the lower the percent you need to save. I also work…and work with people who make exorbitant amounts of money and are financially *d*ependent and must work much later in life than they like in order to support their lifestyles. Remember: it's not what you *earn*, it's what you *keep*…and what you *do* with what you keep.

> *"That man is the richest whose pleasures are the cheapest."*
>
> – Henry David Thoreau –

Independent vs Dependent

To sum up this premise let me explain why I prefer "Heydays" to the term "retirement" and what I mean by dependent as well as independent. The concept of retirement is a product of the Industrial Revolution. Industry owners found a need to replace 65-year-old workers with more productive younger workers.

Therefore, in 1935 the government created social security. Of course, life expectancy in 1935 was about 60! If a worker was still alive at 65, he or she could collect social security and wait around to die. Social security was never intended to be a long-term retirement fund.

With today's life expectancy extended by almost 30 years, the concept of retirement has to change. Many companies now find 65-year-olds to be more productive than younger workers due to improved health, experience and a stronger work ethic. Employers struggle with the "entitlement" issue, when younger workers show up late or don't show up at all, who don't work hard, yet are indignant when called on it.

I, for example, don't plan to completely "retire" until health or death forces me to. I've worked hard; I've loved what I've done, and what I'm doing. I feel I've helped people, and I've always enjoyed the people I worked with. Although my first career didn't pay well, I still reached my "Heydays" by age 40, because by then I was independent and worked as much as I wanted. While teaching, I had saved 12.5% of my salary, and I still put 20-25% of my earnings while being a financial advisor into a fund I can access anytime for income. I traveled, mostly within the U.S., owned lake places, and coached my children year-round in sports, something I would not trade for all the tea in China. Also, as you will see, I used debt mostly to attain assets that appreciated.

Therefore, I equate the concept of being **rich** or *having sufficient money* to being **independent** and in control of my life and destiny. Webster defines *dependent* as "controlled, directed, subordinate, servile, slavish"…in other words, relying on a job, something, or someone other than yourself. Interestingly enough, the second part of the definition is: "attached, reliant, beholden, subject to"…in other words, "indebted."

There is *good debt* we'll call "leverage," or attaining an asset we couldn't otherwise afford, that goes up in value; and *bad debt*, where we owe money and probably pay too high an interest rate on an asset that goes down in value, such as a car, which is probably the worst investment you'll ever make. It's the most expensive thing you will ever buy that will eventually be worth nothing.

Student loans are good debt. They give you leverage on the investment of your future. But like any debt, they should be kept to a minimum. The less debt you have when you graduate from college, the sooner you can rid yourself of it and work toward being independent, not dependent. A recent poll shows about 50% of college students move back in with their parents when they graduate. I am happy for them that they have accommodating parents. Or are the parents just "enabling," as a headline at the beginning suggested? I assume most graduates would rather be moving on with their lives, would rather be independent, or as Webster said: self-reliant, free, and autonomous. I was giving a class on money to fifth graders and I asked them if, when they graduated from college, they would rather have their own place or move back in with their parents. They laughed.

Webster went on to define independent as: "solvent, well-to-do, in easy circumstances." In other words, living well and well within your means. A common misunderstanding is that people with money are obsessed with it. I work with people who have saved and those who haven't. I find people with sufficient savings don't need to worry; it's those people in debt and living paycheck to paycheck—unfortunately much of the population today—who are obsessed with money.

"Nowadays people know the price of everything and the value of nothing."‡

– Oscar Wilde –

Love of Money

Money. $. Since it makes the world go 'round, let's take a closer look at money and put its importance in perspective. According to Webster, money is "a medium of exchange." At one time, and still in some rural areas today, livestock—pigs, cattle, fish, crops—were traded or exchanged for other necessities. In some countries still, things such as beads represent "exchange rates," with larger or more colorful beads representing more value for exchange. Basically, like beads, the paper our "money" is printed on is worthless. We cannot grow money on trees. So our government, via the U.S. Bureau of Printing and Engraving, originally held objects such as gold, which has intrinsic value, in the U.S. Mint as a standard against which coins and bills were made and then sent to the Federal Reserve Bank, which in turn made them available to banks, which in turn made them available to businesses and individuals. Using these coins and paper as an exchange for things we want has become recognized around the world as the most "convenient" system.

People originally placed an actual value on the coins and paper because we were told we could exchange them at any time for the gold held in Fort Knox. But soon, governments around the world discovered that gold was, like, really rare. So it was more convenient to back it with something easier to come by, namely "nothing." Gold is still, supposedly held in "reserve," but we can't even get in to see it. So, as Dave Barry said in his *Money Secrets*, for all we know, Fort Knox is filled with Cheese Whiz.

So, be careful about what you desire. As I've already said, money, like plastic, in and of itself, is worthless. It's more a matter of something representing a value that you can exchange for something you *want*, or, hopefully, *need.* Money is only the "medium" between the two. Whatever you do, do not "love" money (unless you're really a fan of Cheez Whiz™). At this point in your life you possess the education from your school days, which can now be exchanged as a skill somebody perceives as having value. That skill has real value, while money has only the perception of value. So, rather than love money, appreciate the skill you have obtained through education and will develop through experience.

*It's not how much you make;
it's how much you keep.*

Reaching the Premise...Finally

So now, in turn, you are going to exchange "work" for "money." Remember, it's not how much you make, it's how much you keep to "exchange." In turn, you'll exchange money for the stuff you "need," or in most cases, "want." I'm suggesting that you exchange some of this $ for independence, the most valuable thing you, fortunately, have the privilege of buying (since you can't buy love, of course). Some of you will make a lot of money; some of you will not. It doesn't matter. It's learning to live within your means, right from the start, before digging yourself a hole or getting caught in a trap you can't get out of that matters. I would suggest, again, that enjoying your job is more important than how much it pays, and nimbly put forward the premise that **RICH=INDEPENDENCE.**

Questions

1. Are you doing things in your life to be dependent or independent? Give some examples of what you're doing and/or what you should be doing.

_____

_____

_____

_____

_____

_____

_____

_____

2. Do you define yourself or judge others by "money," i.e., what you/they wear, cars you/they drive, etc? What do you think about this?

_____

_____

_____

_____

_____

_____

_____

_____

3. Do you have a "dream" for how you want to spend leisure time in your Heydays, i.e., like my having a place on Lake Vermilion in the back of my mind whenever I considered spending or saving? What is your dream, even if it's speculation right now? Will this provide motivation for you to be "fiscally responsible" now? How?

_____

_____

_____

_____

_____

_____

_____

4. If you had to pick your ideal first job or career, what would it be? What would it lead to? And how could this fit into your Heydays when you are "financially independent"?

_____

_____

_____

_____

_____

_____

_____

5. Is there a danger in today's society of "loving money"? What does this mean to you?

_____

_____

_____

_____

_____

_____

_____

_____

_____

_____

6. Do you buy the concept, "It's not how much you make; it's how much you keep"? Explain.

_____

_____

_____

_____

_____

_____

_____

_____

_____

_____

7. Do you believe in the premise **Rich=Independence**?
Why or why not?

_____

_____

_____

_____

_____

_____

_____

_____

_____

_____

_____

_____

_____

CHAPTER 3

FINANCIAL LITERACY

Lucky or Unlucky?

Tom is an old friend of mine. Tom always felt he lived "the good life." He was lucky…he thought. Now when he visits me at the lake he whines about the job he'll head back to on Monday… one he isn't satisfied with or by…but one he can't leave because at his age he can't make that kind of money anywhere else. He's doomed to labor at that unfulfilling job for years to come. He buys lottery tickets in case he gets lucky.

Here was Tom's first car:

then:

then:

then:

Tom's first boat,

then:

then:

Tom has had jet skis, snowmobiles, 4-wheelers. He still has three motorcycles. All these things represent what could have been Tom's retirement account. Tom makes a lot of money and lives *each year* on more money than he has accumulated in his only income-producing asset—his 401k. This is Tom's birthday cake from his kids, who had no college accounts. Tom is one of many "unlucky little boomers" who have spent most of their money on assets that depreciated. They saved little. They planned, I'm sure, to pay themselves, not first…but last, which means by the time they paid everyone else, there was little if anything left for themselves. Now people like Tom will be dependent for years…with their distant "Heydays" growing more and more distant.

On the other hand, here is me with a couple of "lucky boomers" (my soccer co-coach Bill and his wife Linda) in front of their sauna on a pristine lake near the Boundary Waters in northern Minnesota. They didn't have high salaries, yet they retired at age 50 with no debt and enough retirement income to not "work" if they didn't want to. Of course, because he was good at his job, he now works on his own terms as a consultant for his old employer and she works "off-site" at their lake home as many hours as she wants. They were *smart* enough to save at least 10% of their earnings all their lives, *disciplined* enough to live within their means, *happy* to put their two children through excellent schools, and *wise* enough to pick a remarkable financial planner to put it all together.

> *"It wasn't raining when Noah built the ark."*‡
>
> – Howard Ruff –

Will you be lucky or unlucky? We have many clients between the ages of 30 and 45 who have lifestyles within their means and are paying themselves regularly, and we can predict when they will be financially independent. But with the federal government reporting a negative, a NEGATIVE, savings rate, I am afraid we are working with a small, if successful, minority…probably pretty close to 20% of the population.

So what about you? Will you follow in the footsteps of the dependent 80% or the independent 20%? You've possibly had the bad luck to have had poor role models: boomers on down who have been purveyors of a consumer-oriented, possession-obsessed society with high debt and low savings…definitely with retirement dreams deferred and drying up.

But, luckily, you have the advantage of time. So, let's talk "financial literacy." As Robert Duvall said, "It's not something you're born with." It is "…learned behavior."

So what follows are the basics of what you need to know to create a successful financial plan. This core knowledge can be best represented by the "Financial Pyramid."

> "You've got to be careful. If you don't know where you're going, you might not get there."‡
>
> – Yogi Berra –

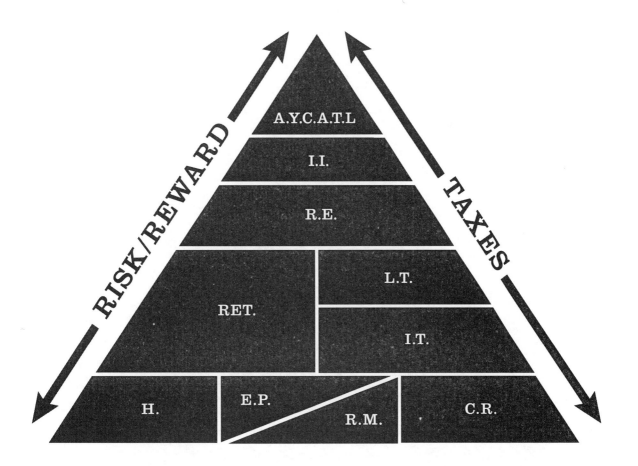

Basics for a Financial Plan

In building a pyramid you want a strong base, because if the base crumbles, the pyramid will fall apart. The farther up the pyramid, the more reward potential, but also the more risk, so it is best if you focus on the base first, then work your way up, gradually taking on more risk.

Besides "risk," on the side of the pyramid, is "taxes." You always need to pay attention to taxes. The more you pay in taxes, the less in your pocket. It may not seem fair, but people with more money are more apt to get professional advice and, subsequently, pay a lower percentage of their income, net worth, and estate distribution to various taxes, although they gift more to charity.

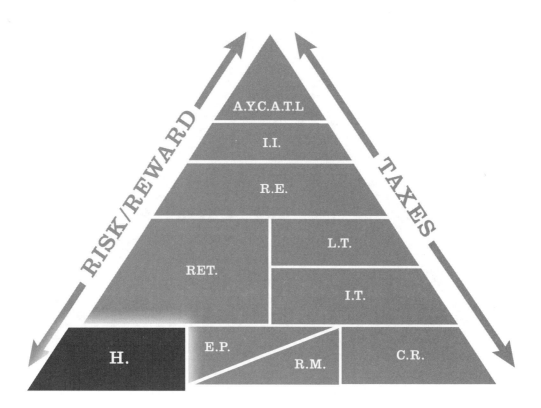

H = Home Ownership

We all need a place to live (since hopefully we won't live with our parents forever). Ownership is generally better than renting because you are building equity. To get started, you will need leverage (debt) because (unless your parents are extremely accommodating) you probably will not have the cash to buy a home outright. This should be considered "good debt," because if you "buy right," not at the top of a market cycle, the home will appreciate.

If you have too many school loans or too much credit card debt, however, you may not qualify for a home loan or be able to handle a home mortgage. Eventually, when you can buy, and as your family begins and grows, you can sell and put your equity into a larger, probably more expensive home, as you'll see I did, each with even more appreciation potential. Make sure your income is commensurate with the mortgage payment so that you can live within your means and still keep a comfortable cash reserve so that you won't go deeper into debt to, say, replace a furnace. Make sure you are able to pay yourself at least 10% of what you make toward retirement, and even more for future college/education expenses if you have children.

When interest rates are *rising*, you are best off locking into an interest rate. If you *know* you are only going to own a home for a short period, say for five years, it is fine to do a 5-year ARM (Annual Renewal Mortgage) with payments amortized (scheduled) over 30 years. The rate will be lower for those five years, but then will jump, probably 2%, each year after to a maximum of maybe a 5% increase. So, if you don't sell within five years, in the long-term you will probably end up paying more because your rate will have grown higher than the locked rate would have been. You can refinance, but then you will be paying closing costs…thousands of dollars…again. So the strategy of an ARM has potential rewards, but risks as well.

A house will appreciate over time if bought at the right price, in a good location, and financed properly.

It's safest, especially if you do not know how long you may own your home, to lock into a 30-year mortgage. You will pay more interest than on a 10 or 15-year mortgage, but your payment will be lower, allowing you add more to cash reserve, retirement funds, and other priorities like a college fund. Hopefully these accounts will grow faster than what the difference in rates between a 10/15-year mortgage and 30 saves you in interest. After all, the banks are giving you a lower rate so they get their money sooner, investing it and planning on a higher return themselves.

When interest rates are dropping, 1-year ARMs are great. If you can find a mortgage broker you trust, you can refinance frequently without closing costs. The broker will get a commission, but that's okay as long as your payment drops. Watch for rates to bottom and lock in long-term before they rise. Unfortunately, this, like the stock market, is not always easy to time.

Although a home should appreciate over time if you bought it right, in a good location, and financed it appropriately, beware there are always risks associated with owning real estate.

You're not entitled to more house than you can afford.

A strong temptation will be to buy more house than you can afford. Don't get carried away. It's easy, I know. The problem many buyers have gotten themselves into recently is to use a 1- or 2- or 3-year ARM to keep the payment lower, but when the rate jumps at the end of the ARM, they can't afford the payment. In a worst case scenario, people take out home equity loans against the appreciation in the home (usually to buy scat) and then they have to sell a house they can no longer afford and the house may depreciate due to demographics, market cycles, whatever…and their mortgage is higher than the market value of their home. It's happened in the past somewhat, but, sadly, is prevalent today. The number of foreclosures are sharply rising.

Most important: Be realistic. You're not entitled to more than you can afford!

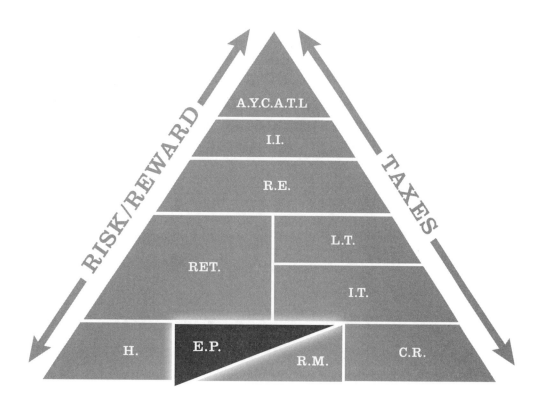

EP = Estate Planning

As soon as you start accumulating assets (i.e., a home), it is a good idea to write a will. An estate plan, whether via a will or trust, like insurances, is really risk management: you are protecting against the effects of the worst possible thing from happening. If you are single, where do you want your assets to go if you die? If you are in a relationship, registering non-retirement assets JTWROS (joint tenants with rights of survivorship) protects each other: if one of you dies, the survivor owns the asset. What if you die simultaneously? Where do you want assets to go? Once you have children, establish guardianship and choose a trustee to handle your children's inheritance in case something happens.

When you get married or have committed to a significant other, you will probably want to make your partner your beneficiary on your retirement accounts. Then if (or when) you die your partner will be able to set up a beneficiary IRA and not be forced to receive the distribution and pay taxes on the proceeds. If you make the beneficiary your estate or a trust, the entire account may be taxable all at once and at a higher rate, as well.

It is also a good idea when you have children to list your contingent beneficiaries as "*per stirpes,*" which means that, down the road, if, heaven forbid, a child who has children predeceases you, his or her share will go to his/her children. This ensures you are not unintentionally disinheriting grandchildren.

Do not make your "estate" the beneficiaries of your life insurance or retirement plans.

Remember: beneficiary designations are good because they do not go through probate (a will) or any estate settlement… but that makes it very important to set them up properly and review them.

Later in life, you may want to replace your will with a revocable living trust (RLT) but a simple will should suffice until you have more significant assets.

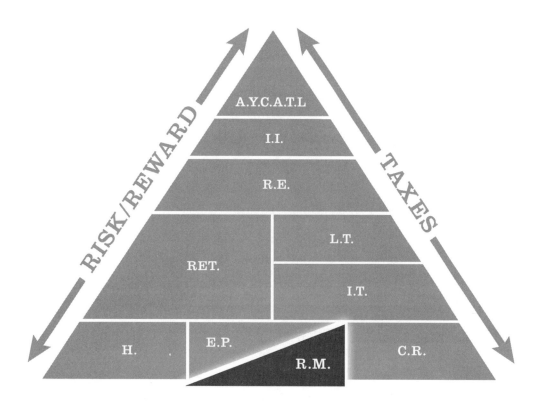

RM = Risk Management

Risk management is a euphemism for insurance. Please make sure you insure your car, your home, and your health. Failure to do so may result in your having no financial future at all. Get a referral for a casualty insurance agent from someone whose judgement you trust, and, hopefuly, your employer will provide health insurance.

Life Insurance

You do not need life insurance until someone is dependent on you for income. So you probably don't need life insurance until you are married, or own an asset like a house with someone. Do not let someone *sell* you a whole or universal life policy to start.

Term insurance to start – when someone is dependent on your income.

Term insurance is relatively inexpensive when you are young and in good health, especially if you are a non-smoker. Term is simply pure insurance, with no cash value. It gives you the most coverage at the least cost, for a specified period of time. Consider getting a 10-, 20-, or, if you're young, even a 30-year level premium policy.

You only need whole or universal life insurance, which has a "cash value" component, when there is a reason to own insurance all your life. Typically when you retire, you should be self-insured…but you might want whole or universal life insurance if 1) you have very high income, do not qualify for a Roth, and have your debt under control, with cash reserve and retirement funding all taken care of; and/or 2) you have an estate large enough to be taxed on both income and estate levels (currently estates over $2 million).

Regarding reason #1, you can "over-fund" your life policy, building up as much excess cash value as the government allows. This excess cash grows tax-deferred and can be borrowed at low or no interest. First, you may draw principal—the premium you have paid with after-tax dollars—and then withdraw the cash value. Since the growth is a loan, there are no taxes. It is a good Roth substitute if your income disqualifies you from doing a Roth. The perfect example of who needs this is a professional athlete. He or she may make exorbitant amounts of money, yet can only get a relatively small percentage of their salary into a retirement account, which they cannot access until the normal retirement age of 55 (rather than a forced retirement from sports of maybe age 30-40 for an athlete), and they don't qualify for a Roth IRA. They can build up excess cash in their life insurance policies, which usually carry high death benefits to protect a spouse or someone else, and take income from the policies at any age, without penalties or restrictions, because it is not an "IRS Qualified Plan."

Regarding reason #2: permanent life insurance can be used at death to provide liquidity to pay debts or estate taxes so nothing has to be sold at an inopportune time. Term insurance gets too expensive when you are older. If gifting to charity is a goal, life insurance can be used to replace the gift to heirs. There are significant tax benefits to this planning, as well.

Disability Insurance

Hopefully disability insurance will be a benefit with your job. If not, or if you become self-employed and have a family, strongly consider insuring against being disabled long-term, even though it is an expense you would rather ignore.

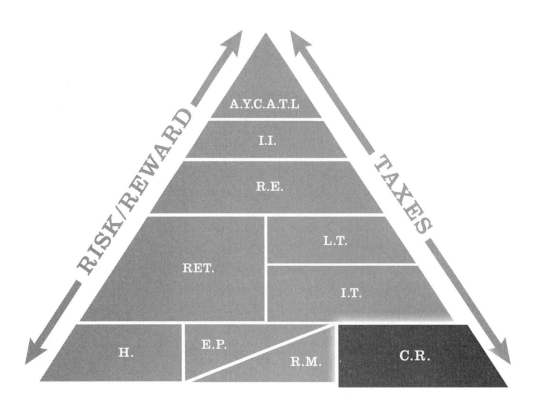

CR = Cash Reserve

This seems simple, but is actually somewhat difficult to determine. How much cash should you keep on hand? The old wisdom says not to invest in anything long-term until you have in the range of 3-6 months income in a reserve account. The rationale is that after 90 days, a long-term disability policy will kick in. Actually, everyone has a different comfort level and this strategy might be fine later in life when, after reading this, you get all the aspects of a financial plan in place.

To start with, you need to: 1) start building a comfortable cash reserve by saving part of each paycheck and, eventually, when you have what to you is a comfortable "cushion" in the bank, start a monthly bank draft to a mutual fund money

A cash reserve is for emergencies.

market, if only $50 a month; *along with* 2) paying down any debt you have; 3) covering your risk management; 4) paying yourself at least 10%, probably via a salary reduction, from the plan you have at work for long-term needs like retirement; and 5) building an education fund if you are lucky enough to have any little tykes crawling around. Living within your means, means you cover all your objectives *before* you spend money on *wants*.

> *Living within your means...means you cover all your needs before you spend your money on wants.*

You can use a bank (interest-earning checking, savings, or bank money market), a credit union or mutual fund money market for a cash reserve...all are "fixed principal" products. Over time, a mutual fund money market should pay the highest interest rate.

It is probably a good idea, especially once you own a home, besides building a cash reserve, to set up a home equity line of credit or similar account to cover short-term emergencies. These loans are much more attractive when interest rates are low since usually they are based on the prime rate. They are tax deductible if the collateral is your home. This could prevent you from having to liquidate another account you would rather not. Just pay it off as quickly as you can, especially when rates are high. The interest rates on these float with the prime rate.

> *You should be less concerned with the return (interest rate) than you are with the principal being "fixed" in a short-term investment.*

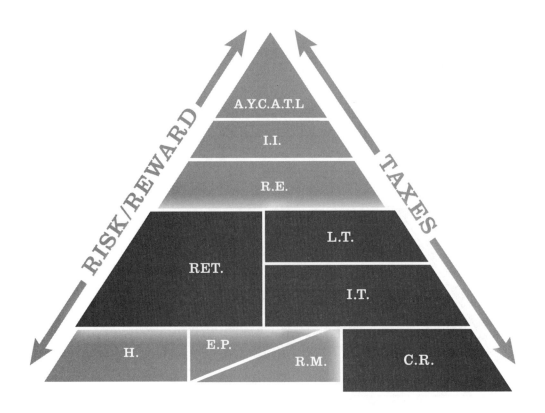

INVESTMENTS

[for Retirement Plans and Non-Retirement Accounts (NQ)]

Basically there are only three time horizons to consider in investing: 1) immediately liquid (cash reserve); 2) intermediate term (1-5 years); and 3) long-term. Depending on your age, situation, and temperament your retirement accounts could be managed intermediate to long-term, probably a combination.

It is time now for a brief lesson on what a FIXED investment is and what a GROWTH investment is. "Fixed" means you have loaned an institution your money (*loanership);* "growth" means you have purchased something (*ownership*) and hope it has appreciated—gone up in value—when you sell it.

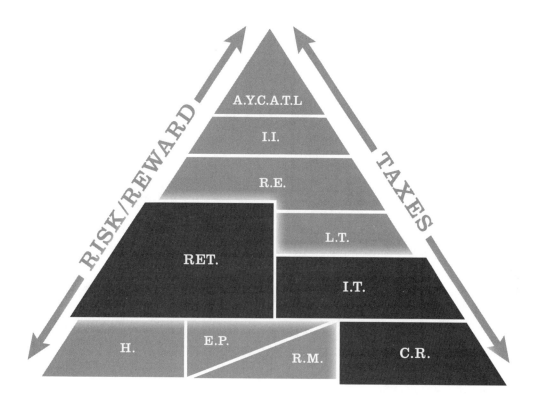

Fixed
Loanership

You can fix two things: 1) *Principal* or 2) *Interest*. A *fixed principal* investment is used for liquidity or cash reserve. You don't really care as much about the return (interest) as you do the security that it will be there and not worth less (sell at a loss) if you need it. The trade-off is that when you loan…like a bank…your money, the institution is going to use it and make more money than it'll pay you. You accept this in exchange for the security of the principal being liquid and readily available and fixed. It cannot go down in value. You don't want too much in this "fixed" situation because the bank uses your money to buy stocks, bonds, real estate, or loans it out to others (or back to you) and earns a much higher rate of return in the long-term. Therefore, you need your "short-term" money, i.e., a cash reserve in this situation, but not your intermediate or long-term money. When the principal is fixed, the interest rate you receive will vary depending, actually, on how much the institution needs to make on the money you loaned to them (their profit margin).

The other thing you can *fix* is the *interest rate.* You can loan your money to a local or federal government, a company, or an institution for a period of time, say 10 to 30 years. They will guarantee you a return (interest or also called a dividend) for that period. This is called a bond and if you hold it until maturity you received the dividend all along and your money back at the end. If you sell the bond before maturity, it may be worth more or less than when you bought it.

Very few people understand the relationship between interest rates and bonds. It's really quite logical, actually. The challenge is not in the understanding but in the remembering. It must be counter-intuitive as the relationship is inverse: as interest rates go up, bond prices go down and vice-versa. Here's why…

Remember, a bond is a "debt" instrument. So I loan $100,000 to ABC Co. and they promise to pay me 6% or $6,000 every year for 20 years, the length of the bond. This is a "fixed income" vehicle. This assumes the bond is not called (canceled by the ABC Co.) and ABC Co. doesn't default (go bankrupt).

But after two years, something comes up and my objectives change and

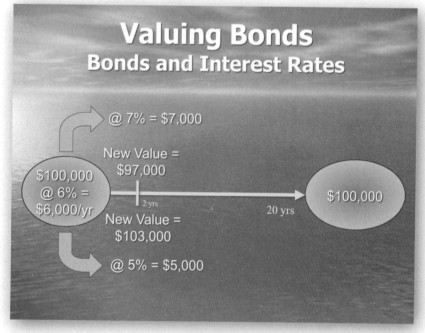

Fig. 3.1

I no longer want the income. I want to sell the bond and use the cash. If interest rates have gone up and you could get 7% ($7,000/yr) now on a new $100,000 bond, if I want you to buy my bond, which is not as good (only paying $6,000/yr), I'd have to "discount" my bond (sell for less). So the bond price would go down.

On the other hand, if interest rates had dropped and you could only earn 5% now, or $5,000/yr, on a new $100,000 bond, my bond is better and you'd have to pay me a "premium." So the bond price would go up. This is illustrated in Figure 3.1.

The duration, or how much time is left on the bond, would naturally be a factor as to how much the discount or premium would be. You wouldn't pay me as much a premium if there were only two years left of a higher return than if there were 18 years left.

So when the Fed changes interest rates, the fixed-income portion of a portfolio may be affected. The NAV (net asset value) of bond funds with longer durations may fluctuate more than those with shorter durations. Figure 3.2 demonstrates this:

Value of a $1000 Bond When Interest Changes 1%

Interest Rates *Rise* by 1%

Duration of Bond	Percent Change	Expected New Price of Bond
1 Year	-1%	$990
5 Years	-5%	$950
7.5 Years	-7.5%	$925

Interest Rates *Fall* by 1%

Duration of Bond	Percent Change	Expected New Price of Bond
1 Year	1%	$1,010
5 Years	5%	$1,050
7.5 Years	7.5%	$1,075

Fig. 3.2

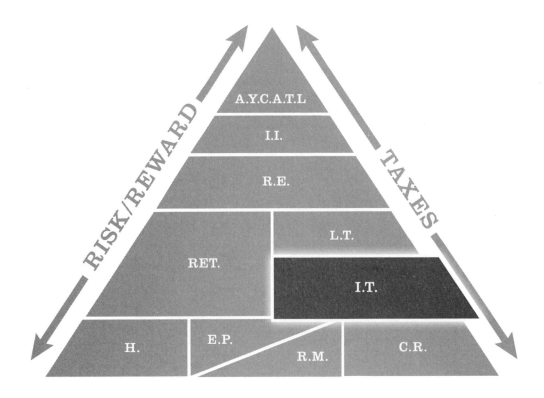

IT = Intermediate-Term Time Horizon

This may seem confusing at first, but just remember the purpose of fixed principal is liquidity or cash reserve, and the purpose of a bond is fixed income. You may want to purchase a bond or bond fund at your age because the dividend is higher than the interest on a fixed principal account, such as a bank savings account, due to the liquidity risk. That is, it may be worth less if you do not hold it to maturity, and under the right circumstances, it may be worth more when you sell it (an example of a risk/reward relationship).

Bonds or bond funds are frequently used for short or intermediate time horizons because of lower volatility.

The closer you get to accessing a joint or retirement account for income, the more likely you will utilize fixed income vehicles. Investors frequently use a bond or bond mutual fund as a short to intermediate time horizon investment because it has less risk, primarily in terms of volatility, than a growth-oriented investment. Under current tax law, interest or dividends on a fixed investment is taxed at the rate determined by your income...so no tax advantage, unless it is a *tax-free* (muni) bond fund, which usually pays a lower interest rate, but may have a higher "equivalent" rate since it's not taxed. Muni's are most attractive, therefore, for people in high tax brackets.

LT = Long-term Time Horizon

Ownership

For long-term investing you'll want to focus on growth. With *growth* investments, nothing is fixed...so there is more risk... and more potential. There are two things you want to grow: 1) the amount of what you own, i.e., number of real estate properties, amount of mutual fund shares or stock shares; and 2) the value of what you own (appreciation). So on the original Financial Pyramid, the sides had "risk/reward" and "taxes." As we move up the pyramid, the higher the risk and the more we look at tax benefits. A good example is that where I said earlier interest and dividends on fixed investments are taxed as "ordinary income," currently you will pay significantly less on the gain or appreciation on an asset you owned and sold. This is called a capital gain and under current law, if you were in a 25% Federal tax bracket or higher, and owned the asset for longer than 12 months, you would pay only 15% in capital gains tax…15% tax bracket—5% in capital gains. (This could be changed any time by the government.)

Figure 3.3 shows what growth and fixed investments, as represented by indexes, have done in "total return" (dividends plus appreciation) over the last 76 years. Over time, due to compounding (the power of which I will show you a little later), the difference between earning 5% and 10% is remarkable. Notice how many more fluctuations occur in the growth area: Large & Small Company stocks versus Fixed, Bond & Bills—which are similar in return to a money market. The problem is that people are very emotional about their money and therefore do not always act rationally or prudently. They tend to buy when the media exhorts the stock market as good (high)

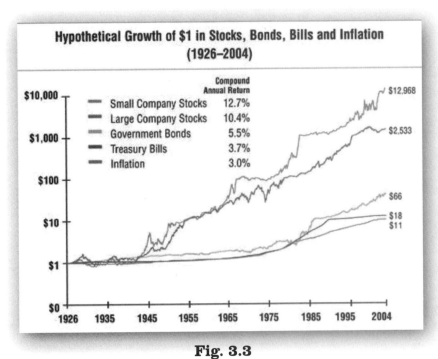

Fig. 3.3

and sell when the media creates negativism and even panic (low).[1] Buy high—sell low = loss. For example people get excited and *buy* when there is a "bull market," where the price of the stock indexes rise; and worried when there is a "bear market," where the price of the indexes drop, and *sell*. Even bears see the folly in this ironically irrational reasoning.

However, most people don't buy low because they don't understand trends, which I expand on in the last chapter, and it's emotionally contradictory: why would I buy something when it doesn't look like I should own it? Of course, the trick is to buy something that's good, that you should own, when the price is low.

Buy high – sell low = loss

The Mutual Fund

Very few people have the time, training, or discipline to research investments such as stocks or real estate. That is why the mutual fund was invented. If you let professionals make the buying and selling decisions within a fund, you're able to purchase shares in hundreds of companies for as little as $25 a month. The mutual fund is a remarkable invention, allowing investors with little money to get the same level of diversification that was previously only possible with the wealthy.

1. I expect the fundamentals in this book to be timeless, but in recent history, 1999—1st Q of 2000, we experienced the highest inflows into the stock market in history when the market was relatively the most overvalued, ever—buying high! Then when the recession hit, massive outflows as people sold low, losing much of what they had gained in the gay 90s. The emotions of greed and fear being the culprit. Same in 2007—2008: after 5 years of growth too many people panicked, fearing another Great Depression, and sold, once again losing their gains. They probably won't get back into the market, again, until it "looks good," i.e., high.

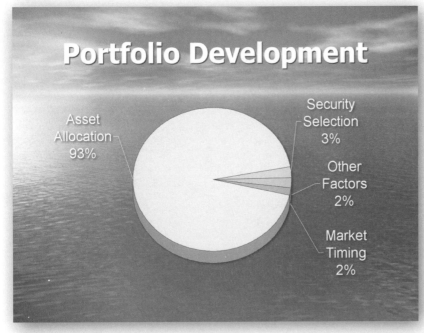

Fig. 3.4

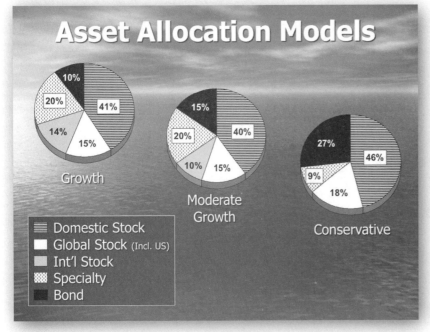

Fig. 3.5

With a mutual fund, you share with other investors by putting your money into a trust fund managed by one or more professionals who have the time, training, and discipline to analyze what you should own. You pick the funds that fit your risk tolerance, so you do not panic and sell low, and these managers buy and sell stock, bonds, real estate, precious metals…and the like for you. The managers will diversify the holdings by buying different companies, in various industries, among different sectors of the economy…even in various countries around the world if a fund you choose allows international investing. This diversification reduces the volatility in the value of what you own and reduces the risk of loss.

Asset Allocation

With intermediate to long-term investments, you need "asset allocation," which is the art and science of diversification. Past research has shown that asset allocation is the most important aspect in developing a portfolio that provides a solid return over time. See Figure 3.4. 93% of a portfolio's success is due to asset allocation.

Figure 3.5 shows some sample asset allocation pie charts. Notice that in general the more aggressive growth will have a higher percentage in global—both domestic and international—stock. More conservative portfolios will hold more bonds and less international stock.

ASSET CATEGORY	CONSERVATIVE GROWTH 60/40	MODERATE GROWTH 80/20	AGGRESSIVE GROWTH 90/10
Cash & Equivalents	10%	5%	0%
Bonds:			
Intermediate*	5	4	0
Long-term*	15	4	4
High Yield*	10	5	4
Stocks:			
Large Cap Growth	10	9	9
Large Cap Value	15	9	9
Mid Cap Growth	5	6	5
Mid Cap Value	5	8	5
Small Cap Growth	0	5	5
Small Cap Value	5	5	4
Global Growth	4	6	8
Global Value	6	8	8
International Large Cap	5	8	9
International Small Cap	0	4	4
Emerging Markets	0	0	4
Real Estate	0	8	12
Specialty	5	5	10
	100%	100%	100%

* May be tax-free if in a liquid, non-retirement account.

Here are more specific sample asset allocation models:

When you are young you can be more aggressive, especially regarding accounts that have a long-term time horizon, like a retirement or education account. Notice the Aggressive Growth Portfolio has no cash and a very small allocation of bonds. The Moderate Growth Portfolio has an 80% holding in Stock and Specialty, with 20% in bonds and bond equivalents. A Conservative Portfolio will have no more than 60% stocks. Market conditions will always dictate the percentages, as a "managed" account is dynamic, not static. Our company even has a portfolio we call "Preservation Plus," in which we attempt to get a better than CD return with very little downside. How we allocate the portfolio depends on the various

Asset Class Returns

Best → Worst	1996	1997	1998	1999	2000	2001	2002	2003	2004	2005	2006	2007
Best	Large Growth Stocks 25.43%	Large Growth Stocks 34.73%	Large Growth Stocks 38.16%	Small Growth Stocks 43.09%	Small Value Stocks 22.83%	Small Value Stocks 14.02%	Bonds 10.25%	Small Growth Stocks 48.54%	Small Value Stocks 22.25%	Foreign Stocks 14.02%	Foreign Stocks 26.86%	Foreign Stocks 11.63%
	Large Stocks 22.96%	Large Stocks 33.36%	Large Stocks 28.58%	Large Growth Stocks 37.38%	Bonds 11.63%	Bonds 8.44%	Small Value Stocks -11.43%	Small Stocks 47.25%	Foreign Stocks 20.70%	Large Value Stocks 8.71%	Small Value Stocks 23.48%	Large Growth Stocks 9.13%
	Small Value Stocks 21.37%	Large Value Stocks 31.87%	Foreign Stocks 20.33%	Foreign Stocks 27.30%	Large Value Stocks -0.51%	Small Stocks 2.49%	Foreign Stocks -15.66%	Small Value Stocks 46.03%	Small Stocks 18.33%	Large Stocks 4.91%	Large Value Stocks 20.80%	Small Growth Stocks 7.06%
	Large Value Stocks 20.54%	Small Value Stocks 31.78%	Large Value Stocks 18.91%	Small Stocks 21.26%	Small Stocks -3.02%	Large Value Stocks -8.18%	Large Value Stocks -16.59%	Foreign Stocks 39.17%	Large Value Stocks 15.03%	Small Value Stocks 4.71%	Small Stocks 18.37%	Bonds 6.97%
	Small Stocks 16.49%	Small Stocks 22.36%	Bonds 8.69%	Large Stocks 21.04%	Large Stocks -9.10%	Small Growth Stocks -9.23%	Small Stocks -20.48%	Large Value Stocks 30.36%	Small Growth Stocks 14.31%	Small Stocks 4.55%	Large Stocks 15.79%	Large Stocks 5.49%
	Small Growth Stocks 11.26%	Small Growth Stocks 12.95%	Small Growth Stocks 1.23%	Large Value Stocks 4.88%	Foreign Stocks -13.96%	Large Stocks -11.89%	Large Stocks -22.10%	Large Stocks 28.68%	Large Stocks 10.88%	Small Growth Stocks 4.15%	Small Growth Stocks 13.35%	Large Value Stocks 1.99%
	Foreign Stocks 6.36%	Bonds 9.65%	Small Stocks -2.55%	Bonds -0.82%	Large Growth Stocks -19.14%	Large Growth Stocks -16.12%	Large Growth Stocks -28.10%	Large Growth Stocks 27.08%	Large Growth Stocks 6.97%	Bonds 2.43%	Large Growth Stocks 11.01%	Small Stocks -1.57%
Worst	Bonds 3.63%	Foreign Stocks 2.06%	Small Value Stocks -6.45%	Small Value Stocks -1.49%	Small Growth Stocks -22.43%	Foreign Stocks -21.21%	Small Growth Stocks -30.26%	Bonds 4.10%	Bonds 4.34%	Large Growth Stocks 1.14%	Bonds 4.33%	Small Value Stocks -9.78%

Fig. 3.6

conditions.

...ourse when you are just getting started you may not ...ugh to diversify this much. Eventually you will want ...start, use core funds that blend large cap growth and .../small growth and value, and global for your growth ...and money market and intermediate to long-term ...sibly tax-free) for your fixed.

...lass Returns

...end quite a bit of time analyzing Figure 3.6 on ...eturns. The point is that the performance of the ...ou see on the chart vary each year. Nobody is ...ly predict which companies will appreciate the ...mutual funds will perform the best or which ...outperform the others. If you were able to, you ...world. The famous investors, such as Warren ...the intuition and expertise to buy "right" ...eventually selling high.

...to combat a down market, such as most recently 2000-2002 and 2007-2009, is to buy...add as much as possible to undervalued investments. By buying low, you're accumulating more shares, and thus benefiting when they all go up in value.

Dollar Cost Averaging (DCA)

The key to your success in long-term investing will be to select good mutual funds managers and add regularly to as many asset classes as you are able and are appropriate for you. This concept is called "Dollar Cost Averaging."

The best way to build a portfolio is to take the timing risk out and add regularly—probably every month or paycheck—to

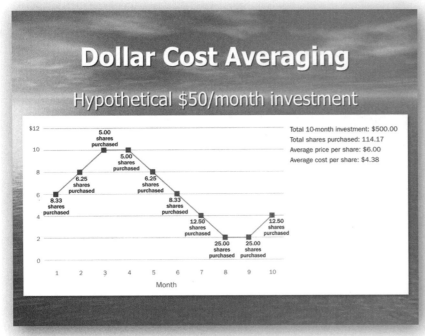

Fig. 3.7

a portfolio. Sometimes you may buy when the market is high, sometimes when it is low, but overall you buy "below cost." Add the most to the funds that are the most volatile…so you will buy the most "low." As you can see in Figure 3.7, you buy fewer shares as the price rises but where the average price per share was $6…your average share cost was $4.38.

I have a large family and many nieces and nephews came to me when I became a financial planner and said, "Uncle Tim, we can't save a penny. We can't afford to pay ourselves anything." I started them all on a bank draft of at least $50 a month. Were they surprised when they didn't even miss the $50! So, we'd increase the bank draft each year. By DCA'ing from their checking accounts each month, they learned to live within their means…and are now preparing for their future… painlessly.

Risk and Performance Analysis

This gets somewhat technical, but even if you're artsy/fartsy, try to get through it:

There are many ways to assess risk. Although past performance should not be used to predict future results, it's a good practice, if you are doing this on your own, to run some kind of software report, like Morningstar's Portfolio Snapshot Report.

With this type of report you can study how a portfolio

of mutual fund holdings performed in the past over, for example, a 3-month, 1-year, 3-year, 5-year, and 10-year time period. So if by 2009, you ran a 10-year trailing return synopsis, you would be able to assess how a portfolio held up during the down market cycle of 2000-2002; and how it performed in the next few years of an up market; and, subsequently, how it performed in the down market starting in 2007.

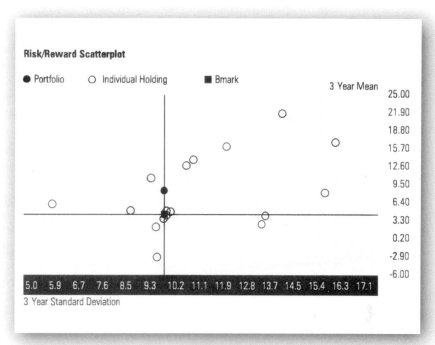

Fig. 3.8

You can also take a look at what the best time period performance was over a 3-month, 1-year, or 3-year period, and the worse 3-month to 3-year period. If the volatility is too great, especially negative volatility, of course, where you might become uncomfortable if the portfolio dropped that much, then you know you need a more conservative portfolio.

You can plug your portfolio into a risk/reward scatter plot that looks like Figure 3.8: The vertical numbers are return percentages and the horizontal is standard deviation (average of how much the value went up and down) over a certain time period. You can choose a "benchmark," such as the S&P500 used in this graph, for comparison. The open circles show where the individual funds fall and the dark dot where the portfolio as a whole fell with respect to the dark square representing the benchmark.

It would be sweet if all funds were in the upper left quadrant, meaning higher return and less volatility. Of course that's la-la-land, but if you're not using index funds and you're

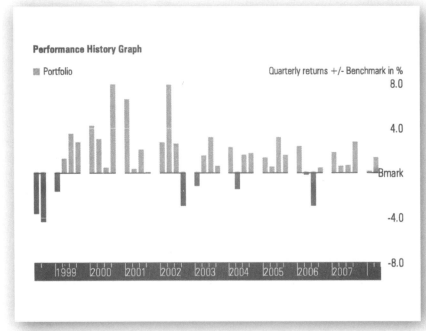

Performance History Graph

■ Portfolio

Quarterly returns +/- Benchmark in %

Fig. 3.9

paying a manager to manage your money (and possibly a financial advisor to help you pick appropriate funds), you either want to have a higher return or less volatility than the benchmark…or, ideally both, for the portfolio as a whole. In this graph the portfolio had a higher return with the same volatility as the S&P 500. A performance history graph such as in Figure 3.9 will show you, visually, the up/down volatility of a portfolio.

If you really want to get technical (engineers? accountants?) you can look at "risk and return statistics" by comparing your portfolio's *standard deviation, mean,* and *sharp ratio* (standard deviation and total return = reward per unit of risk) against a benchmark's for any chosen period of time. You can also determine your portfolio's *alpha* (measures the value added or subtracted by a portfolio's manager), *beta* (standard deviation relative to a chosen benchmark…one being the same deviation; lower than one, less; more than one, more), and *R-squared* (degree of correlation between a portfolio and a benchmark).

You only spend on "wants" after you cover your risk (insurance) needs, are putting at least 10% into a "retirement" fund, and adding regularly to your cash reserve.

If you find a financial planner you are comfortable with, he/she should go over all of these analyses with you.

Factors to Consider

The factors involved in selecting an appropriate asset allocation model for you are:

1) Your time horizon: the younger you are and the more time you have to meet your objective, the more aggressive (growth-oriented) you can be.

2) Composition: percentage in types of investments… domestic, global, or international stock; bonds; or a variety of "specialty" areas such as real estate (not individual properties but investment trusts or partnerships).

3) Style: you may own stock funds composed of large, mid, or smaller capitalized companies. These companies could be paying a significant dividend (value) or putting most of their earnings into research and development (growth). In choosing bond funds, you could choose federal, state, or local domestic bonds (muni's), high-rated corporate bonds, low-rated corporate bonds (high yield), or international bonds. This explanation is over-simplified, but basic.

4) Sector: there are many sectors such as Manufacturing, Service, and Information and these are broken down into many sub-sectors. The managers of the funds will be trying their best to pick companies in sectors that are undervalued (low) rather overvalued (high). With the plethora of mutual funds available today, you will have specialty funds that are not as broadly diversified and may focus on specific sectors.

5) Return Potential versus Risk: the investment world today is highly technical and specific information is readily available. A common technique to measure risk (volatility), as I mentioned, is Beta, which, again, you can find in a report

similar to Morningstar's. A fund's standard deviation is compared to an index over a period of time. If the beta is "1" it has the same volatility as the index…less than 1, less volatility…more than 1, more. The same thing can be done with a portfolio of mutual fund holdings. The point is that if you are going to pay mutual fund managers to manage your money, over time they should be able to do better than an index like the Dow Jones Industrial Average (30 of the largest companies) or the Standard & Poors 500 (500 of the largest companies), and do it with less volatility. You can also measure the beta of the asset allocation of your portfolio, comparing your portfolio with an appropriate index, as I showed earlier.

6) Cost: You are either going to choose what to do yourself or find a broker/financial planner you are comfortable with. If you do it on your own, there are many ways to trade individual issues. Since I'm recommending you get started with mutual funds…you'll be looking at what are called "no load" funds. "No load" is somewhat of a misnomer since there will always be two costs built into the fund: 1) the annual fee that's deducted for the manager(s) of the fund; 2) the annual distribution costs which are the advertising costs in magazines, on TV, etc. which attract individuals to the fund (because you may not be working with a financial advisor who picks the funds.)

If you use a financial professional working off commission, you may be charged either an up-front cost to purchase a mutual fund ("A" shares); a deferred sales charge, which means you'll pay no up-front charge but a higher annual cost for 5-7 years and a declining surrender charge if you redeem your shares in the fund in that time period ("B" shares); an annual charge of about 1% with no up-front charge, and with some funds a one-year required holding period ("C" shares).

Fig. 3.10

You may decide to choose a fee-based planner who does not charge commissions but charges an annual fee which can be a fixed percentage of your portfolio, usually around 1% of the total value, or a "fee for advice" (without management of the funds).

Talk to a reputable planner, maybe via a referral from a satisfied client, and then decide if you are comfortable paying for advice or if you want to do it yourself. Since I'm a financial professional, and, naturally, can justify what I do, I'll tell you the statistic: according to Dalbar Inc.'s Quantitative Analysis of Investor Behavior—2007 (Figure 3.10), the average mutual fund investor achieved an average analyzed return of 3.9% for the 22 years ending 12/31/07 versus an 11.9% average annual total return for the S&P 500 index. This is due to greed and fear: buying high, selling low. With advice from a financial planner you should be able to avoid this. In addition, a good planner should provide the incentive to be disciplined regarding all the elements in a well-rounded financial plan. Do not "cut off your nose to spite your face." In other words, since a good investment advisor should be able to put together portfolios that at least match the indexes, do not lose 8% in return to save 1% in fees.

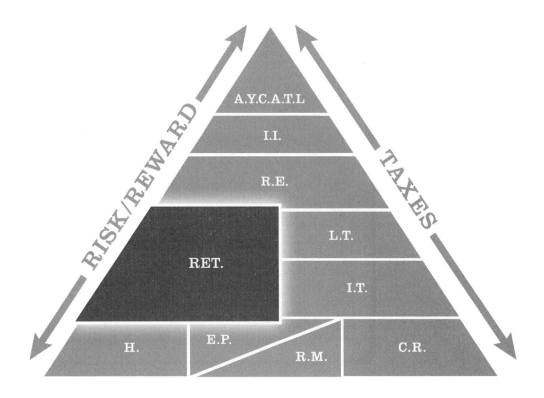

RET = Retirement

Qualified Plans

Qualified plans are retirement accounts, with rules imposed by the government, intended for retirement after age 59½. When you start your first full-time job, if it's a for-profit company you will probably be automatically enrolled in its corporate retirement plan. You'll have to *opt out* if you don't want to participate. If it's a 401k and offers you a *Roth* contribution, invest at least 10% of your salary if the plan allows it. Just do it and learn to live with it, or I guess I should say "live without spending 10%." Yes, it would be nice to be able to spend it...and there will be lots of stuff you will want to spend it on. Believe me, I understand. As a teacher, I had no choice,

> *"Retirement at 65 is ridiculous. When I was 65 I still had pimples."‡*
>
> – George Burns –

as in most government jobs: 12.5% was automatically withheld from my paycheck. If I had had the choice, I probably would have spent it…but, I had a wife, a house and two kids by age 22, besides a dog, two cats, goldfish, and parakeets that always seem to wake up dead. I lived without it and it helped me to become financially independent by age 40. I know retirement doesn't seem like a priority when you get your first job…but since time is the most important element for equity growth, it is best if you make it a priority. Most companies no longer have the old pension deal where, if you stay there long enough, they will put money into a "defined benefit" plan for you. Times have changed, as well. Most of the time people do not stay at a job long enough to establish any kind of meaningful pension income at retirement. If you get a government or union job, you will probably have this plan. Otherwise, you'll have a "defined contribution" plan and it's up to you to fund it.

If they don't offer you the option of a Roth contribution… well, I will give it to you straight: if there is a company match, contribute the minimum to get the maximum match (free money). Then try to complete your *Roth* Individual Retirement Account on your own or see a financial professional. If you still can do more, if your cash reserve is comfortable and you are adding to that monthly…even $50, then go back and do the maximum into the 401k.

I'm stressing the Roth IRA or Roth 401k because: 1) you will most likely be in the lowest tax bracket of your life and so, although the Roth is not "pre-tax" or deductible against your income, the deduction is not as important now; 2) although "after-tax," your Roth will *never* be taxed. Even with all that growth, you'll never pay any tax when you withdraw it. It will provide more income than a taxable IRA or 401k will, assuming the growth rates are the same; 3) there is more flexibility built into the plan for early withdrawal; and 4) under current law there are income limitations regarding contributions to a Roth, so at some time you may not qualify to do a Roth…and the government may discontinue the Roth. To a certain degree the government is mortgaging the future by not giving you a deduction now, but forgoing taxes later.

But…to be straight as I said, if you can't do the Roth as a salary reduction, you'll need discipline to do it yourself outside your job. A salary reduction is the least painful and most likely way to get that money into your retirement account because you never get your sticky little fingers on it. In other words, you'd be better off to do your payroll reduction to a non-Roth 401k than *not* doing a Roth on your own. I guess you just have to know yourself…the most important thing is that you put at least 10% of what you make toward your "independence account." Invested similarly, a Roth will provide more income plus having some liquidity built in, in that you will not pay an early withdrawal penalty on the growth if used for qualified events such as education and first home purchase. The principal— amount of your contribution— is available after 5 years, without tax or penalty, for any reason.

There are other "defined contribution" plans where you *and* the company contribute such as the "Simple" plans. There might also be a company profit-sharing program where the company contributes for you.

If you work for a non-profit institution, you can add to a 403B, which is like the for-profit 401K. Same suggestions as for a 401 Roth: when young add as much to the Roth as you can if they offer it. Frequently you will also have a companion "defined benefit" plan as I mentioned before. Government jobs allow a contribution to a 457, called a Deferred Comp Plan. If you become a highly compensated employee, there are various non-qualified plans your employer can utilize to help you defer taxes until retirement or even eliminate taxes.

If you have no company plan available or are self-employed, you can do the max into a traditional IRA. If you have a plan at work but make under $65,000 Single, $109,000 Married Filing Jointly, you can do at least a partial Traditional IRA, with a current max of $5,000 per person, with a $1,000 catch-up if age 50 or older, and deduct the contribution from income. So no taxes now, until you withdraw funds, hopefully not before retirement. Note: you *cannot* do a Traditional *and* a Roth IRA. You can add to a company plan *and* a Roth, however, as I said earlier. There are income limitations for a Roth also: the phase-out amounts are $105,000-120,000 filing singly or $166,000-176,000 filing jointly.

You can also put up to 25% (a maximum annual contribution level of $49,000, in 2009) of what you make as self-employed into a SEP (Simplified Employer Pension plan), which means if you earn enough you can get more than a $5,000 IRA contribution (both the $5,000 IRA and $49,000 SEP maximums as well as the max's for 401 and 403 and the catch-ups are scheduled to be indexed up in the future. Check www.munkebyfinancial.com for updates).

The money you put into a non-Roth (traditional IRA, 401K, 403B, etc.) qualified retirement plan will be pre-tax now, will grow tax-deferred, but will be taxed at ordinary income tax rates determined by your income when you retire, and penalized 10% if withdrawn prior to the age of 59½. However, there is a 72-T rule which allows for penalty-free withdrawals for early retirement, which could be very important if you get started right away and are independent sooner than your contemporaries, i.e., before 59½.

You can use mutual funds, stocks, bonds, annuities, and real estate investment trusts or partnerships to fund a retirement account. You'll probably have a portfolio of mutual funds to choose from for your retirement plan. Make sure you allocate similarly to the asset allocation suggestions. You may also have the choice of company stock. The recommendation is not to allocate more than 10% of company stock to your portfolio.

The compositions of your qualified retirement portfolio will look the same as for the non-qualified except, since all but the Roth will be pre-tax and taxed as ordinary income when withdrawn (the Roth is after tax and your contribution and the growth is never taxed), we would not use tax-free muni's but taxable bonds instead for the fixed portion. It's also likely that your risk tolerance may be higher and you can be more aggressive because, hopefully, you won't be accessing these funds until you may need income in your

Qualified Retirement Plans

- Bonds
- Stocks
- Mutual Funds
- Annuities
- REITs
- Limited Partnerships

Heydays. As a matter of fact, I strongly encourage that you consider the retirement funds untouchable. Don't be tempted to use them before you're independent…because, remember, you'll pay taxes and probably a 10% penalty! When people leave one job and go to the next, a high percentage of them cash in their retirement plan dollars, usually a 401k, and lose as much as half to taxes and penalty. Either roll the plan you're leaving into the new plan at your new company, or even better, roll it into your own IRA.

Here is a list of all the qualified retirement plans available and current contribution limits for 2009:

	Age 49 & below	Age 50 & over
Company sponsored plans...		
401k/401 Roth	16,500	22,000
403b/403 Roth	16,500	22,000
Simple IRA	11,500	14,000
457 (deferred comp)	16,500	22,000
SEP (Self-Employed Plan)	49,000	N/A
Simple K	11,500	14,000
Individual plans...		
Individual 401k	16,500 (+25% of income to max of $49,000)	22,000+
Traditional IRA & Roth	5,000	6,000

You may not have a choice as to the type of plan available to you since your company may only give you one plan option. Make sure you're doing the minimum amount to get the maximum match, if there is one. Then, as I said, do your Roth, then come back and complete your company plan, probably a 401k, if you are able. Do the 401 Roth for at least half if that is an option.

If you are self-employed, you can do an (Individual) IRA or a SEP, which is now very flexible, allowing you to determine what you contribute each year from 0-25% of your income, to an annual max of $49,000. If you're really doing well, the individual 401k allows the largest contribution. You (and your spouse) must be sole proprietors, however.

A "tax-free" Roth IRA should provide more income at retirement than a "tax deductible" IRA (or 401k, 403b, etc.) if invested similarly.

Non-qualified Plans

Non-qualified means it doesn't fall under the restrictions of IRS qualified plans such as 401ks and IRAs, which have contribution limits and penalties for early withdrawal—before age 59½—unless, again, you use the early retirement 72-T rule. Non-qualified plans include: 1) annuities, which grow tax-deferred, but also are penalized (except under a rule similar to 72-T) if withdrawn before 59½. The growth is taxed as ordinary income. 2) Excess cash values in life insurance, which can be accessed any time, tax-free, by withdrawing principal or by taking loans. Using cash value insurance should only be considered after you've maxed out your company plan or IRAs. However, a common use of life insurance is where, say, you are a foreman or manager, a top salesperson…your company can reward you by buying a life insurance policy on your life. There are many ways to structure this, but generally if you stay there long enough you'll have a cash value in the policy that will be yours and possibly even the death benefit. If structured properly the cash value withdrawals can be tax-free to you.

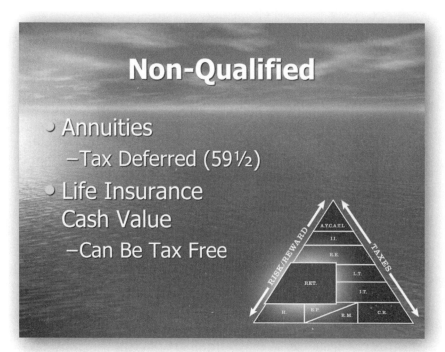

Loophole

(Sort of) a loop-hole: from 2007–2010, a person who makes too much to qualify for a Roth ($105,000-120,000 Single; $166,000-176,000 Joint) can do a "non-deductible" IRA and in 2010 a restriction will be removed that will allow a conversion of the non-deductible IRA to a Roth IRA, regardless of income. Income taxes would need to be paid on the growth, only. Consequently, a person who hadn't been able to do a Roth in the past would, in effect, be able to get their own and their spouse's contributions into a Roth. If he/she only had a corporate plan, like a 401K, this could make good sense. If a person had other IRAs or a SEP, the IRS has a formula that might make this planning detrimental. Check with a good financial planner to see if this strategizing may be appropriate.

10% of income into a retirement plan, at 1st paycheck, and increase each year with inflation. No excuses or you'll be sorry. I guarantee it.

Bottom Line

You cannot rely on Social Security; you will probably have to rely solely on yourself. So do it…and start right away with your first job to put at least 10% of what you make towards retirement and learn to live on the rest.

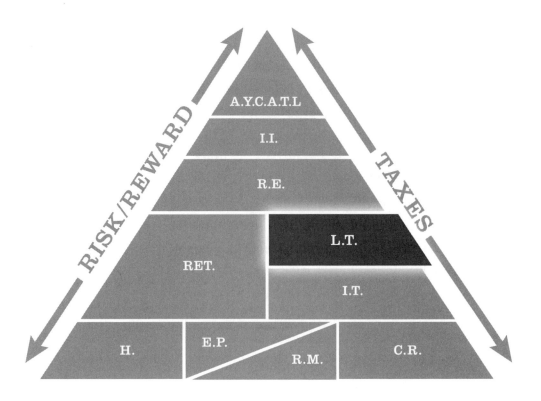

LT: Education Accounts

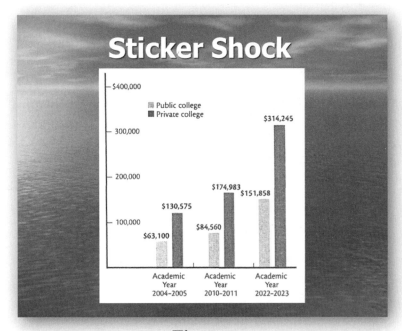

Fig. 3.11

Sticker Shock

If you plan to further your education down the road or if you start having children, you should consider opening or adding to the various tax-advantaged Education Savings Accounts the government currently allows us to use. With the costs of higher education rising at a faster pace than core inflation, if you want your children to have the opportunity to get the best

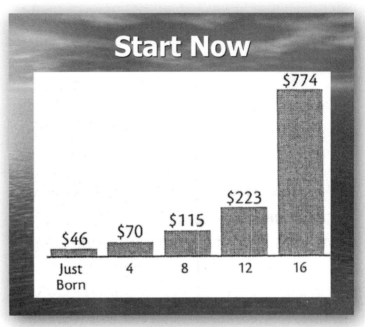

Fig. 3.12

education they qualify for, you may well need to have funds available for them. "Sticker Shock," from The College Board Report (2005), illustrates the current and projected costs of a 4-year education (Figure 3.11).

As with retirement, the sooner you start to contribute the less you will have to put in. Figure 3.12 illustrates this: assuming a 7% annual return compounded monthly, you would only need to save $46 a month from the birth of your child to have $20,000 by freshman year. If you wait until your child is 16, you'll need to put away $774 a month. Of course $20,000 might be what you need for *one year*, so you may need to multiply by 4…which in actuality compounds the need to start early (i.e., $184/month at birth versus $3,096/month if you wait, as most boomers have, until a child is 16).

So make sure you have an adequate cash reserve, do not stop adding to your retirement, but start putting what you can into one of the following plans as soon as you have your baby.

Here is a list of the various education accounts and the benefits/limitations of each as of 2009:

Liquid Accounts: No limitations; taxed at owner's bracket.

Roth IRA: Taxed before 59½ but no 10% penalty if used for beneficiary's education. Your basis (what you put in) was after tax and so is available without penalty after 5 years, but the growth (increase in value) will be taxed if used before 59½.

Savings Bond: Tax-free if used for education. Trade-off is no growth potential but has a set interest rate.

UTMA (Uniform Transfer to Minor Account): No limitations; a gift; taxed at owner's bracket until minor is 18; minor becomes owner at 21.

Education IRA: $2,000/yr contribution max; tax-free if used for any education level.

529 Plan: $12,000/yr contribution max. (Can be accelerated each 5 yrs, i.e., $60,000). Tax-free if used for post-secondary.

Insurance Cash Value: Tax-free withdrawals of premiums, tax-free loans of cash value growth which may be charged interest; must accompany a life insurance death benefit.

- **Liquid** accounts can always be accessed without penalty, but interest and dividends will be taxed annually and a capital gain tax may be assessed, assuming there has been appreciation in the account, when you liquidate. Of course it is difficult to predict what will end up being the most appropriate post-secondary education for your child, thus what the costs, thus how much you need to save in an Education Savings Account, so it may be necessary to use liquid accounts for some of the costs. Loans are always available, but must be paid back. Government loans usually have the lowest interest, with "subsidized" being the best since they do not accrue interest or have to be paid back until the student graduates.

- After five years from each deposit, the principal from a **Roth** is available without tax or penalty and the growth without penalty, but the growth is taxed at beneficiary's bracket if used for education before the owner is 59½.

- **Federal saving bonds** are tax-free if used for education, but have a fixed return with no growth potential. Depending on your risk tolerance and circumstances, you may want some "guaranteed" funds…and it's best to start early enough for the bonds to mature. You're more likely to build a larger education account using mutual funds in the Coverdell Education IRA or 529 plan, which are also tax-free.

- The **UTMA** can be used for education or anything benefiting the minor, not only education. It was more widely used before the advent of the tax-free accounts. It has fewer tax benefits, but the advantage is that the usage is more flexible and there are no contribution limits. It becomes the minor's account at age 21. He/she then is in control of the account when it goes into his/her name. This can be perceived as a detriment.

- The **Coverdell Education IRA** has a low $2,000 maximum contribution, but can be tax-free for any level of education, K-grad school.

- The **529 Plan** allows a larger contribution, $12,000 a year currently, and can be accelerated: $60,000 up front, without the ability to add for 5 years. Obviously the most can be accumulated tax-free in this type of account. The government actually structured this account to allow parents and especially grandparents, who have more assets than they need, to transfer some to these education accounts. If grandparents gift to these accounts, the accounts are best left in the grand-parents' name so the assets won't be considered when applying for student aid. The maximum is currently planned to be indexed up each year. These must be used for post-secondary education, only.

- Since **cash values** in **whole life insurance** products are "non-qualified," principal can be accessed and excess cash value borrowed with no tax. You may be charged interest, depending on your policy.

Start right after the birth of each child to add regularly to a post-secondary tax-free fund.

Many parents today are, unfortunately, putting off retirement to put their kids through post-secondary education. Many stop adding to their plans at work, take loans against their 401s or 403s, or even worse take "premature distributions" (cashing in) from their retirement plans to pay tuition, incurring penalties and taxes as well as diminishing their retirement funds. If you start adding to an education account for your children early enough, you may be able to avoid these pitfalls.

Do not count on student aid unless you plan on having few assets and low income. Your child (or you?) may qualify or apply for grants and scholarships, but you cannot count on these. It's best to save in a tax-free education account and start early so as to have to save less. These accounts are transferable to others.

Graduate-level students qualify for financial aid on their own, so more loans and assistance may be available…but, remember, do your best to keep these to a minimum.

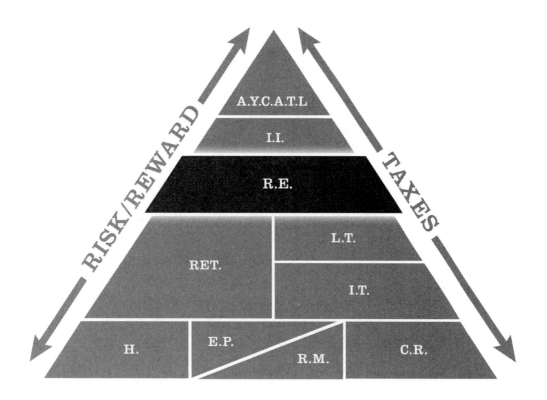

RE = Real Estate

If you "buy right," owning a home, as mentioned earlier, should be preferable to renting due to the possibility of appreciation. You'll see how I did it by always transferring the equity of a home into another worth more, with even more opportunity for appreciation. Remember, "buying right" means not at the top of a market (understand trends), in a good location, and with decent terms in your mortgage. When you are young, getting the lowest rate possible on a 30-year fixed mortgage is probably your best bet, especially when rates are low…but you can check the Munkeby Financial website for other variables related to mortgages.

Real estate is higher up on the pyramid because real estate, if not owned in a mutual fund, has liquidity risk: it is generally a longer-term holding period or you stand a chance of losing money. Direct ownership is like owning your own home. Most of you will not have the cash or collateral to own an office building, hotel, or retail space, so you will have to pool your money and buy shares or units along with other investors. Many REITs (Real Estate Investment Trusts) are in the form of a mutual fund and so are liquid. You can buy shares of the fund and sell whenever you want...being aware of costs and fees.

Non-correlation

An important factor in asset allocation is the non-correlation of assets in your portfolio. In other words, you don't want all your holdings reacting the same to any economic factor. For example, large, mid, and small cap stocks frequently react differently in market cycles. Growth frequently doesn't correlate with value. International stocks don't always correlate with U.S. stocks, international bonds with U.S. bonds, and, of course, bonds with stocks. Utilizing sector rotation, i.e., rotating out of over-valued sectors and into under-valued sectors showing relative strength for a portion of your portfolio, can also help maintain a more consistent performance. Real estate has a low correlation to stocks and bonds.

Figure 3.13 shows what types of real estate might be held in an REIT as managers generally diversify across a broad range of sectors.

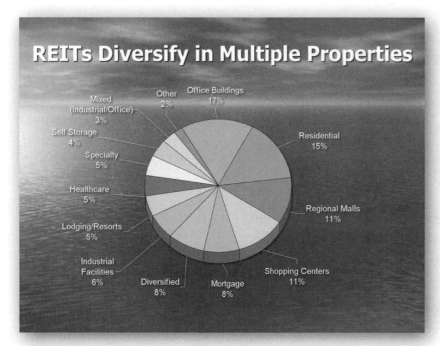

Fig. 3.13

Figure 3.14 shows correlation based on monthly returns and averages for the 25-year period 1979-2004. A value of 1.00 would indicate that an investment moved "in tandem," in other words in the same direction, up or down, and the same magnitude. A value of 0.00 would indicate no correlation, -1.00 opposite movements. You can see how little correlation REITs have with stocks and bonds. Non-correlation is a significant factor in producing a consistent return and reducing volatility.

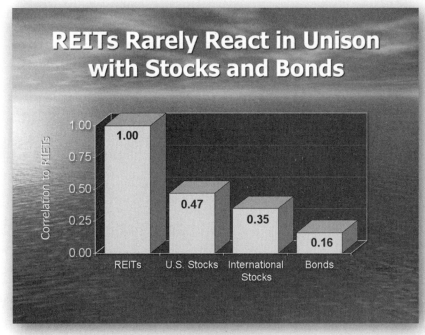

Fig. 3.14

REITs can also be in the form of partnerships or private placements where there is a mandatory and undetermined holding period or you pay penalties to sell early.

Own a home as soon as you can afford it, and diversify your retirement plan when you've accumulated enough value with a 5-20% allocation to real estate mutual funds.

Bottom Line

Do your best to own your own home and, if possible, have a 5-20% holding in your portfolio in real estate through mutual funds. One of the main reasons for holding real estate, probably in the form of REITs, in a portfolio is for non-correlation.

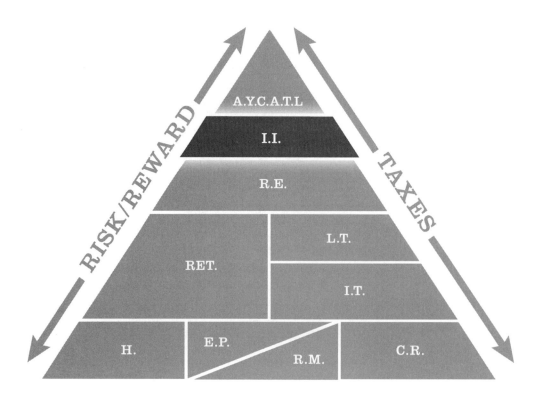

II = Individual Issues

It may seem fun to trade stocks and you may have belonged to an investment club where you researched to attempt to pick a "winner." The truth of the matter is even the professionals have a hard time finding the right stocks to own and you will probably not have enough money to adequately diversify. To begin with, your serious money should be invested in time-tested mutual funds diversified in a good asset allocation model.

> "Don't gamble; take all your savings, buy some good stock and hold it till it goes up, then sell it. If it don't go up, don't buy it."
>
> – Will Rogers –

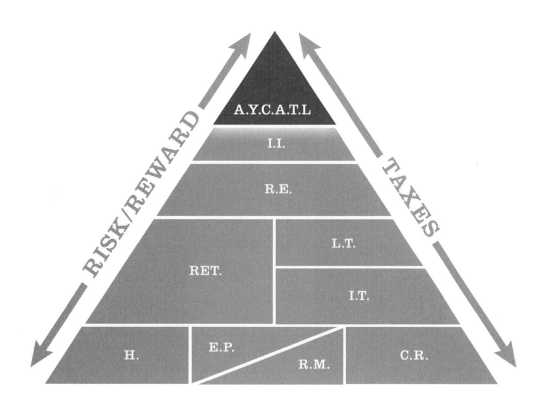

AYCATL = Anything You Can Afford to Lose

As it says, when all your bases (the lower parts of the pyramid) are covered, try anything you like…as long as it does not matter if you lose. I remember a Minneapolis woman invented fake nipples and was looking for investors. I am sure the product attracted many investors' *interest*, but not necessarily their money…? But, who knows? The Breathe-Rite (nose patch) worked if you got in early enough. 3M did start in a garage, but for every 3M there are thousands of Enrons.

> *"Money can't buy friends, but it can get you a better class of enemy."*[†]
>
> – Spike Mulligan –

Play around, if you like, with individual stocks and speculative investments only with money you can afford to lose.

Questions

A. Home Ownership

1. What's the most important concept in buying a house? What temptation should be avoided?

_____

_____

_____

_____

2. What are the three most important considerations about the house?

_____

_____

_____

3. What's probably the most appropriate financing? Why?

_____

_____

_____

_____

B. Estate Plan

1. When and why should you have a will?

_____

_____

_____

2. How should you list the beneficiaries on life insurance and retirement plans?

_____

_____

_____

_____

C. Risk Management

1. Why do you need to insure your car, home, and health?

_____

_____

_____

2. When do you need life insurance?

_____

_____

_____

3. What kind of life insurance should you have initially? Why?

_____

_____

_____

D. Cash Reserve

1. What's the purpose of a cash reserve?

_____

_____

_____

2. Over time, what cash reserve account should pay
the highest interest rate?

_____

_____

_____

_____

E. Short- to Intermediate-Term Investments

1. What are the two things that can be "fixed" in a
fixed investment?

_____

_____

_____

_____

2. What's the relationship between bond prices and
interest rates?

_____

_____

_____

_____

3. Are "fixed" or "growth" investments more
appropriate for an intermediate-term time horizon?
Why?

_____

_____

_____

_____

_____

F. Long-Term Time Horizon

1. What's the difference between "loanership" and "ownership"?

_____

_____

_____

_____

2. What mantra is fundamental to making money in ownership? What mistake do most people make? (e.g., greed and fear.)

_____

_____

_____

3. What is a mutual fund? Why was it invented?

_____

_____

_____

4. What is asset allocation?

_____

_____

_____

5. What is dollar cost averaging? What does it accomplish?

_____

_____

_____

6. Why is investor return over the last 22 years 3.9% vs. the S & P 500 index return of 11.9%?

_____

_____

_____

7. What's the best way to combat a "down market"?

_____

_____

_____

8. What perspective should you have to protect yourself against the effects of greed and fear?

_____

_____

_____

G. Retirement Accounts

1. What's the minimum percent of your income that you should contribute to your retirement account?

_____

_____

_____

2. When should you start contributing? What should you do each year?

_____

_____

_____

_____

3. What's better when you're younger: a Roth IRA or a Traditional IRA (401K or 401b)? Why?

_____

_____

_____

_____

4. Unless you have a government or union job, who's going to be responsible to fund your retirement?

_____

_____

_____

5. What's the 72T rule? Why is this potentially an important rule for you?

_____

_____

_____

H. Education Accounts

1. When should you start an education account for your child?

_____

_____

_____

2. What's the advantage of Education IRAs and the 529 Plan?

_____

_____

_____

3. What's the difference between the Education IRA and a 529?

_____

_____

_____

_____

4. Who else can add to these accounts for your children?

_____

_____

_____

_____

I. Real Estate Investments

1. Since you probably won't have the money to invest in commercial real estate, how can you accomplish ownership?

_____

_____

_____

_____

2. Why should you consider real estate in your portfolio when you have accumulated or are adding enough to diversify?

_____

_____

_____

_____

3. What's a good percentage of your portfolio to have invested in real estate?

_____

_____

_____

_____

_____

J. Individual Issues

1. What's the concern with owning individual stocks when your portfolio is relatively small?

_____

_____

_____

_____

_____

K. Anything You Can Afford to Lose

1. Why are individual issues and AYCATL at the top of the pyramid?

_____

_____

_____

_____

_____

MOTIVATION

Philosophy

A guy I know from high school said to me once: "You know, I don't get you. You drive these piss-ant cars (actually, a newer high-mileage Honda or Toyota and an old truck or van); your kids all drive those old cars…Jeez, your wife even cuts your hair. You put all your money into houses, some crappy cabin with an old Chris Craft inboard, lakeshore…however you waste your money. I am smart. I've got this little house so I can buy a real boat (a new 33-foot ocean-going vessel), nice cars (Escalade, Lexus, and Boxter), a couple of wave-runners, a snowmobile for myself, wife and each of the kids. While you run off to that cabin up in the bush (actually red and white pine), I take my little lady to France, Greece, the South Seas…"

This guy is a prime example of what is now being dubbed as a "poor little boomer." Of course my crappy little cabin appreciated nicely, as did all my cabins and lakeshore. I even sold my "old" Chris Craft for more than I bought it for. One Honda Accord passed to the children and was still going at 240,000 miles when we had a wreck that did it in. We still managed an inexpensive trip each winter, maybe not Europe, but to Mexico or a fun U.S. destination. Many of the boomers put all their earnings into "things" that depreciated, and the *little* house which could have provided my high school friend a lot more appreciation, relatively, is mortgaged to the hilt to help finance the "scat" that may now be worthless. I'm not saying you cannot "live life to the fullest." Every person has a different idea of how to make their life meaningful and I'm not saying you shouldn't buy anything that depreciates or that you have to finance. Just don't sell your soul…in my book it's not "things" that make you happy, anyway. As they say, "you can't buy love" (even if you had a million dollars), but you can "buy" independence. But you must be strong and not fall prey to marketing predators who want you to *want*…to spend beyond your means…the primary trap being credit cards. Remember: *zero balance* each month or you're spending more than you have, creating a potential black hole of debt you may never get out of and thus never be able to save…to pay yourself.

Spend within your means.

"*If you're already in a hole, it's no use to continue digging.*"‡

– Roy W. Walters –

Psychology

If you invest emotionally, you will buy high, i.e., when the market is up and it looks good; and sell low, i.e., when the market is down and looks bad. In other words, you will lose money. The Cycle of Emotion (Figure 4.1) is a good graphic illustration. As I said, research has shown that the average mutual fund investor achieved an annualized total return of only 3.9% for the last 20 years, while the average annual total return for S&P 500 was 11.9%. This difference was due to buy/sell timing decisions initiated by the fund owner. It's impossible to predict or time the market, so just SAVE regularly and stay invested. Remember, if you dollar-cost-average, when the market is down you are buying more shares. The markets will always fluctuate; just don't *sell* when the market is down.

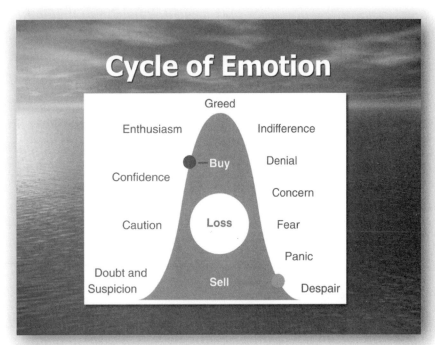

Fig. 4.1

You must buy low and sell high to make a profit. But it's easier said than done because it's counter-intuitive.

Forecasting

"So, how much will I need to have invested to live the way I want to in my Heydays?" you ask. All of you will have different lifestyles. The $75,000 average annual lifetime income (unadjusted for inflation) may seem like a lot for some of you, a pittance for others. But, for a frame of reference, we have already seen that if you had a million dollars after age 50 (by having an average salary, saving 10% of what you earn, starting right away, investing it properly and history repeats itself) you could receive $50,000 (5% of $1 million) a year, before-tax income, and adjust up each year for inflation. Could this help provide you with the opportunity to do what your little heart desires for the rest of your life?

10% of an average lifetime salary = $1m by age 50 if invested properly and history repeats itself.

Inflation

Let's look at inflation, which is often referred to as the "silent thief" because you don't notice it. Ask your parents or grandparents which cost more, their first house or last car? In most cases, it would be the last car. Whew! To keep ahead of inflation, make sure your annual income increases at least by the rate of inflation, your savings increases with your income, and your investments stay ahead of inflation. The only way, by the by, to have done that in the past was to invest in equities…things that appreciate such as stocks, mutual funds, and real estate.

> *"Great moments in science: Einstein discovers that time is actually money."*
>
> – Gary Larson –

Rule of 72

A great "rule" is the Rule of 72 (Figure 4.2): you divide 72 by the expected rate of return to determine how long it takes your money to double. So, look at Figure 4.3. Let's say you have $10,000 and you stick it in a savings account earning 2%. It will take 36 years before you have $20,000. But now look at Figure 4.4. If you were able to get an 8% return, you would have $20,000 in 9 years…and $40,000 in 18 years…$80,000 in 36 years. Notice by increasing your return by 6%, you had 400% more money. That is the nature of *compounding* over time. Einstein referred to compounding as the "8th Wonder of the World." This is why time is the most important element in growing a portfolio.

Let's use the Rule of 72 to look at inflation. If inflation continues to average 3% as it has in the past, it will take 24 years for the cost of living (COL) to double. If inflation is 4%, COL doubles every 18 years, so your latte could cost you $10 and your average pair of bifocals close to $2,400. Some prices increase faster than normal inflation. Gas has doubled about every 16 years, so in 24 years it could be $12 a gallon. The cost of a college education, for example, has increased from an average of $270 a year in 1965 to over $10,000 per year in 2008…much more than core inflation.

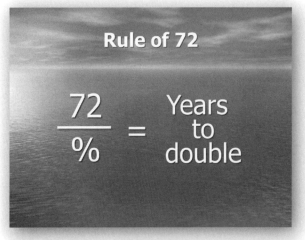

Fig. 4.2

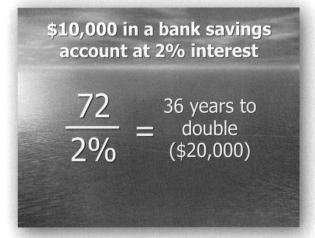

Fig. 4.3

Fig. 4.4

Fig. 4.5

Start Now

So…"How much do I need to save or, excuse me, *pay myself first*, to be financially independent?" Well, let's take a look. Since we don't know what inflation will be in the future, we'll use today's dollars. As I said earlier, you will have to make sure you increase your earnings, what you pay yourself and your return on investments, by at least the rate of inflation.

Let's look at some other numbers and projections. Figure 4.5 shows how much you would accumulate by age 65 if you invest $2,000 each year and earned 8% starting at age 25, versus 35, 45, or 55. What'd I tell you: start right away!

I hope this is sufficiently startling to you. Don't make excuses for not saving…paying yourself. There'll be loads of excuses: school loans, beer, weddings, cars, a house, kids, college…meds, nursing home…Figure 4.6 shows what you'd have to save each

Starting Right Away

Current Age	Years to Save Until Retirement	Retirement Savings Goal	Monthly Savings Needed to Reach Goal
25	40	$1,000,000	**$157**
35	30	$1,000,000	**$439**
45	20	$1,000,000	**$1,306**
55	10	$1,000,000	**$4,841**

All figures assume a 10% annual return on investments and retirement at age 65.

Fig. 4.6

month if you earned 10% and wanted a million bucks by age 65: start at age 25 and $157 a month will do it. Wait 10 years and you need to tuck away $439. Wait until you're 45 until reality sinks in and you better be able to rise above average reality as you'll need to stash $1,306 each month to reach your goal. If you're lucky enough to pull your head out (of the trap?) by age 55, I hope you're really lucky in love or something as you'll need to pack away $4, 841 each month.

The message is pretty obvious. If you start at 25, you may accumulate your million by saving just $157 a month. Just by waiting 10 years, at age 35, you'd have to contribute almost three times as much each month to make up for your procrastination.

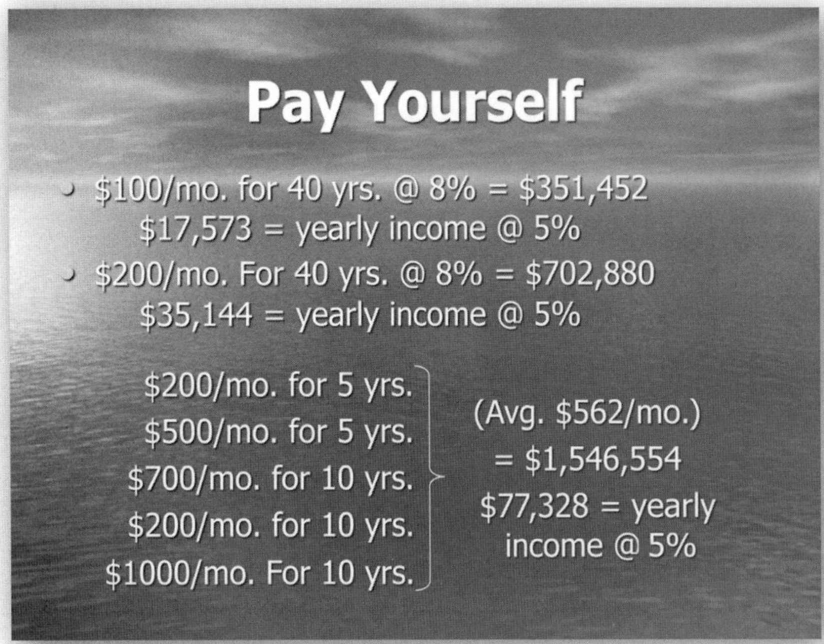

Pay Yourself

- $100/mo. for 40 yrs. @ 8% = $351,452
  $17,573 = yearly income @ 5%
- $200/mo. For 40 yrs. @ 8% = $702,880
  $35,144 = yearly income @ 5%

$200/mo. for 5 yrs.
$500/mo. for 5 yrs.
$700/mo. for 10 yrs.
$200/mo. for 10 yrs.
$1000/mo. For 10 yrs.

(Avg. $562/mo.)
= $1,546,554
$77,328 = yearly
income @ 5%

Fig. 4.7

Projections

Also notice you would have gotten to $1M by saving $157-per month if you had gotten a 10% return. If you would have earned 8% for the same time period, it would have grown to $551,746. Return is second to time in importance.

Of course, if you want to be independent by 50 (assuming you're age 22) enabling you to be contented, self-actualized...doing exactly what you want to be doing to make your life fulfilling, you'd need to average paying yourself $541 each month @ 10% average annual growth or $796 @ 8%. If you wait even one year, the monthly amount needed starts to increase significantly.

Let's say you only pay yourself $100 a month for 40 more years (Fig. 4.7) and get an 8% average annual return: you would have $351,452, which would give you $17,573 in yearly income at a 5% withdrawal rate (x .05). Add social security to that and you will have between $32,000 and $50,000 depending on whether there are one or two of you collecting full or partial.

Save $200, however, and at 8% for 40 years (Figure 4.6) you would have $702,880, giving you $35,144 a year ($50-67,000 with Social Security).

More than likely, the amount you will save will vary depending on career pay, lifestyle, family, and so on. So let's say you start saving $200 a month for 5 years (Figure 4.7). Then you get married and get serious with both of you working, so $500 a month for 5 years. Then up to $700 a month for 10 years as your pay increases. Then kids in college, $200 a month for 10 years but, thank the Lord, kids are on their own… there are some weddings but you do $1,000 a month for the final 10 years. You have averaged $562 a month and at 8% could have $1,546,544 or $77,328 yearly income. That is pretty close to the average income nationally, and, assuming there is still Social Security, you would be at $92,000-110,000.

Pay Yourself

$100/mo. for 40 yrs. @ 10% = $637,633
$31,880 = yearly income @ 5%

$200/mo. For 40 yrs. @ 10% = $1,275,267
$63,760 = yearly income @ 5%

$200/mo. for 5 yrs.
$500/mo. for 5 yrs.
$700/mo. for 10 yrs.
$200/mo. for 10 yrs.
$1000/mo. For 10 yrs.

(Avg. $562/mo.)
= $2,662,009
$133,100 = yearly
income @5%

Fig. 4.8

Return

Of course, as I mentioned previously, the return you get is second in importance to time. So, if you were able to get a 10% return, as you can see in Figure 4.8, you'd come close to doubling your growth and, consequently, your income…or you would be able to be financially independent much sooner. A 2% higher return over 40 years, as shown in Figure 4.9, equaled

**Effects of a
Better Rate of Return**

10% = $133,000 Income
vs.
8% = $77,328

(2% Difference in Return over 40 Years
= 90% more income)

Fig. 4.9

Effect of a Better Rate of Return

Average Monthly Installments Needed to Reach $500,000 in 20 Years, Based on Different Average Rates of Return

Fig. 4.10

a 90% difference in income. You don't have to be Einstein to realize proper investing is significant.

Another way to look at why you need to get the best return you can is to peruse Figure 4.10. The number $500,000 may not be enough for you, depending on your lifestyle, as it would provide $25,000 yearly income (at 5%, without using principal), so double the figures if $1 million sounds more like what you'll need...the point, regardless, should be obvious. As we have discussed in the past, the S&P 500 has a 10.3% average annual return for over the past 75 years. Smaller companies have averaged closer to 12%, but you aren't going to hold only smaller companies, because you need diversification through asset allocation to control volatility. So 12% is probably way too optimistic, but the graph makes the point that the better the return, either the less you need to save to reach a goal, or the sooner you may get there. You need to save three times as much at 4% than 12% to reach $500,000 over 20 years.

Time (and compounding) is the most important element in accumulating wealth. So...start now.

So why not, since I'm young, just invest only in small companies or funds composed of small cap companies? The answer is you have emotions you can't ignore and small caps are very volatile even though their averages are higher. You, as a human being, will experience the variations, not the averages. Yogi Berra, who had so many good sayings…made this point well: "Averages don't mean nothin'. If they did, you could have one foot in the oven, the other in a bucket of ice and feel perfectly comfortable." So beware of the expected volatility in more aggressive investment categories. The point is, you need diversification in your asset allocation. Also, a disclaimer is needed for any return forecasting: "past performance may not be an indication of future results."

The Tortoise and the Hare

Figure 4.11 continues to amaze me. It's the allegory of the tortoise and the hare: you invest $10,000 and in an aggressive investment you get a 15% return for three years, then a -15%, followed by a less remarkable 7%. After the 5 years, you would have $13,961.

As a tortoise you are more diversified and get a boring 7% return each year. After 5 years you'd have $14,026. More than the hare!

So, it's not that you should have all your assets invested speculatively, but aim to be well-diversified in a good asset allocation model to control down-side risk.

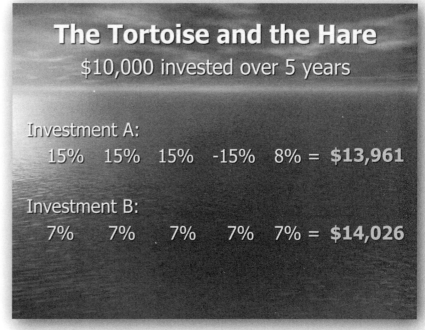

The Tortoise and the Hare
$10,000 invested over 5 years

Investment A:
15%   15%   15%   -15%   8% = **$13,961**

Investment B:
7%   7%   7%   7%   7% = **$14,026**

Fig. 4.11

Historically, the riskier the investment, the higher the potential return (risk/reward relationship). So if you have a long-term time horizon and can emotionally handle volatility, you can afford to be in a more aggressively allocated growth portfolio… and if the investments you choose are well-managed, you should be rewarded…especially if you're dollar-cost-averaging.

Pay Me First

Let's look at another good lesson in starting to *pay yourself first*, right off. In Figure 4.12 Mary is a nice, conservative young woman who had the intelligence to read *If I Had a Million Dollars* in college, and invested $4,000 annually in a Roth IRA from age 22 to 28. But then poor Mary marries a slacker and he spends all their money. So she stopped contributing to her IRA. Bridget, on the other hand, parties, until at age 28 she reads this great book and decides she'd better get serious and does her $4,000 contribution to a Roth IRA from age 28 to 67. So Mary has a total of $28,000 invested before Bridget starts to save her $156,000. Who has more? I know you guessed— Mary (even though you really do not believe it). But true! If they both earned 10% (the average of the S&P 500 for 75 years), Mary would have $1,711,080 at age 67; Bridget $1,452,207. It is very expensive *not* to start *paying yourself* first right off the bat.

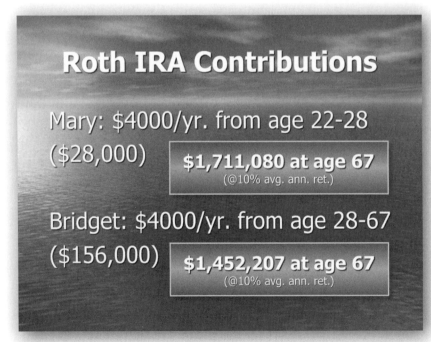

Roth IRA Contributions

Mary: $4000/yr. from age 22-28 ($28,000)
$1,711,080 at age 67
(@10% avg. ann. ret.)

Bridget: $4000/yr. from age 28-67 ($156,000)
$1,452,207 at age 67
(@10% avg. ann. ret.)

Fig. 4.12

The Real Cost of a Car

If you had a million dollars, would you buy a BMW Roadster? Or, let's say you finally have your first real job... you worked hard in school. You deserve it, right? Well, a million bucks is about what it would cost you. "What!?" you say. No way. Well, let's say you had 50 grand...a BMW at $50 thou or a Toyota at $20 thou? If you buy the Toyota and saved the $30,000, let's use the Rule of 72 to see what the BMW actually cost. To keep the numbers even, let's say you could earn 7.2% on the $30,000: 72/7.2 = 10 years to double. So, look at Figure 4.13. By a retirement age of 67, the BMW would have cost you $480,000...and would probably be a pile of rust.

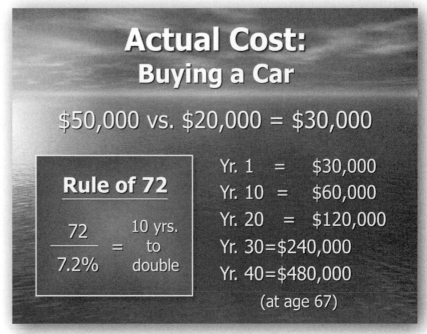

Actual Cost:
Buying a Car

$50,000 vs. $20,000 = $30,000

Rule of 72

$$\frac{72}{7.2\%} = \frac{10 \text{ yrs.}}{\text{to double}}$$

Yr. 1 = $30,000
Yr. 10 = $60,000
Yr. 20 = $120,000
Yr. 30 = $240,000
Yr. 40 = $480,000
(at age 67)

Fig. 4.13

Well, at least it was not a million dollars, you say. Okay, look at Figure 4.14. Let's assume you don't have $50,000 cash, much less a million. So you finance the car over 5 years at 6% interest. If you had saved the difference between the 50 thou and 20 thou monthly payment and earned 8% you would have $42,680. If you let that grow for 40 years and got 8%, you would have $927,702...pretty darn close to a million bucks. If you had gotten a 10% return, you would be well over a million. I have nothing against BMWs, Mercedeses, Lexuses, Cadillacs, or the like. I just want you to know what those wheels will eventually cost

Actual Cost:
Financing a Car

$20,000 → $385/mo. @ 6% x 5 yrs. = $23,100
$30,000 → $577/mo. @ 6% x 5 yrs. = $34,626
$50,000 → $962/mo. @ 6% x 5 yrs. = $57,720

Invest $577/mo. @ 8% x 5 yrs. = $42,680
($962-$385)

$42,680 x 40 yrs. @ 8% = **$927,702**

Fig. 4.14

you…and be aware of how fast those wheels depreciate. Since the purpose of a car is transportation, the primary difference between an expensive car and a reasonably-priced car is what you may *want*, and what you actually *need*. Again knowing the difference between wants and needs is the most important determiner of living within your means…which in turn will determine whether you are independent, hopefully early in your life, or possibly dependent *all* your life.

Purchasing a Car

Let's say you've decided to buy a new car. Since a new car depreciates so drastically immediately after you buy it, you buy a low-mileage, one-owner car that is clean and, after you had it checked out, you know has been well maintained. You have put aside $12 grand and that is the max you are going to spend. You've done your internet research and know pretty much what you can expect to find for that price. In other words, you know what value you should receive for the cash you've got.

So you hit your favorite lot, liking the 30-90 day warranty that hopefully assures you're not buying somebody's problem. You find exactly the car you've wanted, except it has special

> *"Americans believe in life, liberty, and the purchase of happiness."*
>
> – Nathan Dungan –

rims, an up-graded sound system with a 5 CD changer, an auxiliary input, and some other "extras" that are very attractive. The cost of the extras is $3 grand and probably more than they should cost, but, man are they cool. So…you **need** the car, you **want** the extras. So have you now expanded your definition of "value?"

According to an article by Jay Palmer in *Barons* (4-1-02): "In the U.S., sales of luxury vehicles rose 800% between 1996 and 2000 compared with a 5% rise for ordinary vehicles and light trucks." Do you think their income rose 800%?

The salesperson suggests that you use your cash to purchase the car and you can put the extras on your credit card. Easy solution, you think: I've only spent what I wanted, and I can make payments on the extras. The use of plastic, not hard cash, has expanded your sense of "value." It's too easy. With the use of credit cards, it's way too easy to lose sight of "price for value," and we pay too much for what we need and fall prey to our learned weakness for "wants." Your parents were much freer with money than their parents, whose spending habits may have been affected by the Great Depression. This has created a sense of entitlement: "I don't need to earn and save the money to buy something…I can have it anyway." And, too often, generous parents continue to bail their kids out…a detriment to both sides.

So if you use the credit card logic long enough, you build up substantial debt. If you only make the minimum payment, you dig a hole that gets deeper and deeper as the debt grows with unpaid interest…you've used up any cash reserve you've got, and you can't build it back up. You can't add to a college account, you can't add to your 401k…you're stressed, obsessed with money due to the lack of it, your health can suffer…is this really what you want!? Keep that credit card at a ZERO BALANCE or you're living beyond your means. Period!

If you have to finance part or all of your auto purchase, make sure you still add to your liquid and retirement accounts. If you can't, buy a less expensive car and stay within your means. "0%" financing is attractive, but usually only available on new cars. Don't let it lure you into a car you can't afford.

Okay, a little on the lighter side. When we were younger, my wife and I always had one newer model, good gas mileage, cheap car (especially when we lived in the country and I commuted to work), and an older work vehicle, like a truck or carry-all. The problem was my wife ended up having to drive the old work vehicle. For a while, that was a 5-speed manual one-ton company truck a friend had actually given to us. One day my wife, not wanting to shift into first, rolled over the railroad tracks by our farm. A young cop stopped her and was going to ticket her for not stopping at the railroad crossing. She looked hard at him and said, "You get in here and shift this beast and see if you'd stop at the crossing when no train is coming!" He smiled sheepishly and let her off.

So our second autos have improved over time as my career did, but I still refuse to pay anywhere near $50,000 for something that would eventually be worthless, no matter how badly I may *want*. But for those of you that really like cars and *want* exciting, not what in your mind is mundane, I'll confess and you will get the point. I always wanted a sports car. I remember one fine summer morning I was killing (spraying) mosquitoes at a really nice house and the husband drove off to work in a little MG. I said to myself, "If I ever have to drive to an office I might as well make the drive fun." It took me a while but I now have a third vehicle. When I first saw a Toyota MR2 Spider, I really liked the mid-engine look. It reminded me of a much more expensive…mid-engine Lamborghini…I do have a good imagination. But they were still over $30,000 and you had to wait forever to get a new one and no one was selling their used ones. Well, I've given up on motorcycles, and besides driving to an office, still, I go back and forth between town (Mpls.) and the lake (Vermilion) frequently. The only foreign car dealership in my neck of the woods is Toyota, in Virginia, Minnesota. So last spring I checked on used MR2s. They quit making them in 2003, so I didn't know what to expect. Well, there were only three available in Minnesota, but they wanted around $20,000 for low mileage 2000 and 2001 models, which is all that were available. My Scottish/Irish genes resisted. But I followed them, two at dealerships and one private party, all summer. They dropped the price a little, but not much. Come September, I contacted the private party, and he said he had been storing a 2000 in a neighbor's garage since he had moved to a condo…so he was willing to sacrifice for about $14,500. Then I checked with a dealership on another 2000 and they said they would match the price! But the Carfax said the right fender had been repaired and painted…so they came down to $13,500! I checked with the other dealership and their car had fewer miles and was one year newer (a 2001). At first, they said there was no way they would match $13,500. So I said too bad, after I drove it, because it was spotless and I wanted this one, but…? As I was getting into my car to leave, the salesman (seriously) came running out and said the manager had relented. So I got the car I wanted. I really never thought I'd get that car for that price, especially with really low miles: it had been stored every winter. The used car manager cried that he was "giving it away," but they assumed they were either going to have to store it all winter or send it off to a warm country auto auction, at a loss for sure.

Now, I know why current owners hang onto their Spiders: it's a great car. I assume the ones I followed weren't selling, because Toyota doesn't make them anymore. Well, I don't really get that, because by my logic that should make them more in demand. Only time will tell, but I betcha' I can drive that

"Midship Runabout" for 3-4 years (although I may just keep it forever) and sell it for more than I paid for it…of course, I'll sell it in the spring or summer.

Buy smart. Not just cars, but especially big ticket items. I always ask, "Is that the best you can do?" Not confrontational…and usually they can do better…and so do you.

Maslow, Again, and a Fulfilling Life

Let me interject something: in my Heydays I figured that my flight to fulfillment would include combining my two careers…teaching and financial planning…thus I'd be giving classes for high school and post-secondary students, hoping to persuade you to seek a fulfilling life, and stay clear of financial doldrums.

I've even asked myself the question: Why do I get a kick out of speaking to young people about money and their contentedness in life? Is it pretentious? Because I am contented myself? What I've come up with is similar to Spalding Gray, the philosopher that suggested we all visit morgues: As I get closer to my life expectancy (maybe everyone would want to feel this way) I would like to feel I left the world a better place for having had the privilege of living in it. If reading this book helps any of you to have a happier, more fulfilling life, I have left the world a better place. Corny?

So writing to you seemed like a good thing to do. Money, being the agent for exchange for the things we need…including independence, has to be an important element. Just remember (how can you not since I've repeated it a million times) that being rich does not mean having the most money (remember—in and of itself it is worthless) but doing what you want to be doing with your life. I'm sorry if you think I'm being pretentious in using myself as an example, but, as I said, at least I am practicing what I preach. I am doing exactly what I want to be doing…not because of the money I *made*, but of the money I *kept*.

> If you want happiness for an hour, take a nap.
> If you want happiness for a day, go fishing.
> If you want happiness for a year, inherit a fortune.
> If you want happiness for a lifetime, help somebody.
>
> – Chinese Proverb –

I alluded earlier to the sharing of monetary success with those less fortunate than myself. I focused on trying to get you to a point where you and your family are taken care of…so you can move up Maslow's ladder and include more altruistic ambitions in your life. A big part of my financial planning practice was always charitable planning. I did pro-bono presentations for charitable foundations in bigger cities as well as small towns…showing how people (as well as my clients) with taxable estates can leave money to causes of choice within their own communities, without jeopardizing, if they chose, what is left to family.

If you're so inclined, a portion of your income can be gifted to charitable causes. There are, of course, tax benefits to this kind of planning, not to mention the intrinsic benefits. Also a portion of your estate can be left, testamentarily at death, to charitable causes.

Again, to practice what I preach: most of the profits from this book will go into a Charitable Trust funding the Munkeby Family Donor Advised Fund. Each year the fund will make gifts to causes of my family's choice. At my wife's and my demise, my children and grandchildren and great-grandchildren…will continue to advise on annual gifts to causes of their choice.

A reputable financial planner can help you with this process if you're interested and if appropriate. If your parents or grandparents have more than they need, suggest this to them. It teaches everyone in the family the true value of money.

Does helping others to have a better life help you to have a better life?

Questions

1. What is the best type of assets to own?

_____

_____

_____

_____

2. What's the best way to avoid trying to "time"
the market?

_____

_____

_____

_____

3. What percent income can you safely take from
an investment without drawing down principal and
probably still able to increase income over time to
keep up with inflation?

_____

_____

_____

_____

4. How can you have a million dollars by age 50–55?

_____

_____

_____

_____

5. What three things do you have to be sure happens
to keep ahead of inflation?

_____

_____

_____

_____

_____

6. What's the Rule of 72?

_____

_____

_____

_____

_____

7. What's the most important element in
accumulating wealth?

_____

_____

_____

_____

_____

8. What's the second most important element?

_____

_____

_____

_____

_____

9. Summarize the meaning (the bottom line) you should extrapolate from all the graphs?

_____

_____

_____

_____

_____

10. What do you think about charitable planning and even a Family Donor Advised Fund?

_____

_____

_____

_____

_____

CHAPTER 5

MY WAY

I'm going to use my life, to date, to show you how I achieved independence earlier than most, not because I think you should do anything like I did, but to show you how even a confused Irish kid growing up being told he was Norwegian (who got his pickle in a pickle and was married at 18) could do it…and if he could do it, so can you. The odds are in your favor because you're young and it's not too late, as it is for many in the generation(s) ahead of you.

This is me with my mother on the shore of Lake Vermilion. I was born to Patricia Wagner and my genetic father, Mac McGinty, who I was told was a brawling, drunken Irishman and whom my mother divorced before they even lived together. Bob Munkeby, a very conservative, mild-mannered Norwegian, married my mother and adopted me at age 2. I didn't know he wasn't my biological father until I got married at 18 and saw my baptismal certificate. My mother was Scottish and frugal and did not believe in a free lunch or any "entitlements"…I had to *earn* everything I got. When she found a good buy on sale—a dress let's say—she would hang it in the living room, like a piece of art, and show it off, bragging how good of a deal she had gotten. Of course, shopping thriftily is an art of sorts…mostly a lost art, I'm sorry to say. Of course, I couldn't have done what I did without her fiscally responsible upbringing.

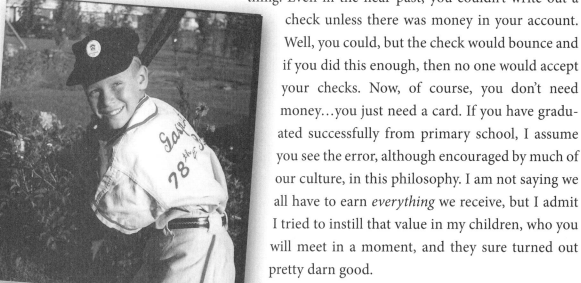

This is me at age 12. See that bat? I had to do chores to earn enough money to buy the bat. Back in the olden days, before credit cards, you had to actually have money to buy something. Even in the near past, you couldn't write out a check unless there was money in your account. Well, you could, but the check would bounce and if you did this enough, then no one would accept your checks. Now, of course, you don't need money…you just need a card. If you have graduated successfully from primary school, I assume you see the error, although encouraged by much of our culture, in this philosophy. I am not saying we all have to earn *everything* we receive, but I admit I tried to instill that value in my children, who you will meet in a moment, and they sure turned out pretty darn good.

There is a value system attached to money. Nathan Dungan, in his book *Prodigal Sons and Material Girls (How Not to Be Your Child's ATM),* defines financial values as "beliefs and priorities that guide financial decisions." To be financially independent you may have to reflect on and alter your current financial values. I caution you, again, about "entitlement": the philosophy that people expect things to be handed to them whether they have earned them or not. It has invaded the workplace. Workers show up late, don't show up at all, don't work hard, yet are indignant when they are called on the table and made accountable. Make sure you get a job or career where you care enough to work hard and try to excel. Even if your first job isn't the greatest, if you do not apply yourself, you'll never get to the right one.

This is the used bicycle I was given by my parents, which got me around the neighborhood pretty well. And below it, this is the bike I bought from doing a paper route, mowing yards and shoveling driveways. These wheels along with three, yeah, wow… **three** speeds! It got me out of the neighborhood and around town…giving me a taste for freedom, you might say. That's when I first realized I could buy independence and while this may seem old-fashioned, because I earned that bicycle, it was tucked away in the garage every night, not lying out in the yard, rusting. Isn't that the fundamental in living "green"? Taking care of things, things both big and small?

I got my first job at the age of 14, selling concessions at old Met Stadium where the Twins and Vikings played. Interestingly, a client of mine has worked concessions all his life, lived within his means, saved 20% of what he earned, and has well over a million dollars at age 50.

The reason I got the job was to have my own wheels by 15. (Back then you could get your permit at age 15 and your license right after.) Here they are, on a Cushman Super Eagle bored out for extra horsepower. Of course, as you Harley drivers are scoffing at "**horse**power" and the colorful fringe, it really wasn't horsepower I was after. I would cruise the city lakes and that backseat was usually occupied. Yes, indeedy, it was "chick power" I was after…back then. And now even more freedom to roam.

My next job, in addition to selling pop, hot dogs, and peanuts, was killing millions of mosquitoes working for my friend's dad's pest control company. Of course, I now know we also killed bushes, trees, and probably some small beasts. However, it provided me with funds to buy a set of wheels with a roof over my head—a rusty '49 Plymouth—although it suffered some in the "chick power" department.

Freedom and independence: since I didn't have to beg to borrow the family car, I was much more on my own.

In my next job, I learned the value of commissions, selling women's shoes, and purchased a 1965 VW Bug, my first wheels reliable enough for my first road trip to Yellowstone National Park. Whew. Talk about being free: the first big road trip. My new-found freedom, ironically, helped attract my most feisty and final chick, Mary. She unfortunately, (or fortunately, as it turns out) was pretty good lookin'…looked like this one night. Here is

my mother's face when I told her we were pregnant and getting married. Actually, they became great friends. Not very good planning, however, as I was in my first year at the U of MN and Mary was still in high school. But we showed 'em we could cut the cake and I did graduate, and 40 plus years later we are still cutting the cake. This is one good example of why I'm not telling you to do it "my way." Although it has worked out for Mary and me, it doesn't for most who get married that young…whatever— just do it your way.

Unfortunately, Christopher Jon was born premature and died two months after we were married. Everyone said, "Too, bad. You wouldn't have *had* to get married." We never felt that way. I figured I did not *have to* get married. I *chose* to. Although our parents did not try to prevent the marriage, they just said, "You're on your own. (Which I pretty much had been, anyway.) Good luck."

Then, of course, one day Mary, while we were on a vacation, looked like this. The next, like this. Yup. Very good planning. Still in school…but we had been ready for a baby so here is Eric at about 18 months behind our new VW Bug, which used to be a relatively inexpensive car, new, yet held its value, and in front of our…not trailer, but mobile "home." It was my first lesson with leverage,

location and appreciation. Leverage because although I could not afford to pay cash for either the car or the "mobe," I financed them both on the same loan at a low rate over seven years and the payment was cheaper than rent. "Location" because I bought the mobe for $3,100 and was lucky to get it on a lot in a mature-treed park in the middle of Bloomington, a thriving suburb. After having our own place (rather than an apartment), we sold it for $6,000. To get this in-demand location, the buyer had to pay this price. So even though I didn't own the lot, the only way for a buyer to get in this park was to buy an existing mobile home: thus location, the most important thing in real estate, and appreciation…it went up in value and gave us the down payment for a sweet little house in Edina Morningside, a sought-after neighborhood with these cute smaller houses, and lots of kids for Eric to play with, adjacent to the "country club" district. I'm sure you've heard: if you have a smaller home in a neighborhood of larger, more expensive homes, their value brings up the value of your home.

We sold the mobe and bought the house after I graduated and got my teaching job. I loved teaching, specializing in improvisational theater and creative writing. Not the subjects you'd expect to lead to a financial planning career. But if I had not been a good teacher, I doubt I would own a financial planning company now, or be writing to you.

Mary looked like this one night (not bad, right?). Here is Emily. This time at least I was out of school and had a career. I need to make a point here. 12.5% of my salary went automatically into TRA (Teachers Retirement Account). I had no choice; I was lucky. If I could have taken the money, I probably would have…and spent it. Because I couldn't, when I left teaching I had a great start on my retirement. You're probably not going to be as lucky. You're going to have to discipline yourself to *pay yourself first.* As I've made the point, the sooner you start, the better. *Time* is the most important element in compounding…even more important than your *return*, as I've shown you.

We got tired of city living and moved to the country, squatted, actually…meaning we lived for free in this old, turn-of-the-century farmhouse in exchange for caring for and riding the owners' horses so they stayed domesticated… the horses, that is. Not a bad gig. We had purchased our home in Edina for $18,000; sold it for $30,000 and stuck the money in the bank. Didn't earn crap…it would have done much better in mutual funds, but for the first time in my life we had a cash reserve, and it relieved a lot of the financial pressure of living paycheck to paycheck.

We didn't want to spend any money on the house so the furniture was all out of the dump. In the 60s and 70s people were throwing away "old" furniture—now trendy and called "antiques." We decorated with parts of farm machinery and used barn-wood for stairs, bookshelves and the like. Heated with wood. Made the bathroom look like an outhouse. A student of mine painted a big pink elephant on Em's bedroom wall. I guess I am telling you this because it will always be my favorite house and we barely spent a penny on it. It taught us we didn't *have* to buy extravagant items to be comfortable and happy.

Here's my favorite picture of the two of us. What makes it a good picture, I think, is that there is a degree of pensiveness in our faces. We'd left the farm, and

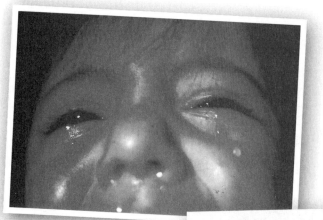

taken teaching positions in Bogotá, Colombia, S.A. This picture was taken at my folks' cabin the day before we left for South America.

One day a year into our South American adventure a nun handed us a 3-day-old baby and asked, "Do you want her?" What d'ya say? You can see what she had to say about it. This is Mary holding Alexandra on the Caribbean Coast where we were living with an Indian tribe, waiting for Alex's visa to the U.S.

When we finally got back to the States the only thing we could afford was another abandoned farmhouse. We bought this one. Mary was not happy to bring her new shiny baby into it, however. So it got a major remodel that we did ourselves…summers, of course. We learned our second lesson in trends…in this case trends in real estate: if you have heard the term "hobby farm," they were just becoming popular…and a few miles down the road they were building Canterbury Downs—the racetrack. I'm going, "So we got 30 acres, barns, corrals, the Minnesota River which our property bordered…with a new horse-trail that ran for 30 miles…if we fix this place up, might not somebody really want it?"

I don't know if you're aware of the old wive's tale that you will get pregnant right after you adopt? Well, here's a wife to prove it. I knew something was different this time…yup, twinners. Adriann and Erin…and almost triplets with Alex just a year old.

Okay, "All good things come to an end"…or, to quote another cliché, "Does a new door just open?" Declining enrollment hits Minnesota schools and I get the "pink notice." So we sold the farm and moved. We had purchased the farm and 30 acres for $40,000. We sold the house and barns and half the land to a horse guy who wanted a hobby farm for $120,000. The 15 acres on the river with this view for $75,000. We moved into town and bought a house for $90,000, on several wooded acres, including marshland, near Ridgedale a block off Highway 12, soon to be I-394. I-494 was called "The Strip." So I figured I-394 would become a strip, too. Another trend?

Let me expand a little more on location in real estate and trends in any investment. When I bought the hobby farm, the term had just been coined. Everyone, including my wife, thought I was crazy to buy an abandoned farmhouse. Like the trend that started a couple of years ago to move to the city and live in lofts, the trend back in the 70s and 80s was to move away from the city to the suburbs and to the country. If a real estate agent got a listing with an acre and a shed, it was a hobby farm. So combine the early stages of a trend with location: a good house with acreage near a racetrack on a river with horse trails…you have property that is in demand and will appreciate. But it's best to recognize the trend before it's popular, so you can buy it *right*.

The location of the new house on I-394 didn't seem like a good location to my family and friends. But the same property on the I-494 strip would have been closer to $1 million than $100,000. But with 394, a new highway near construction, and

an upscale shopping mall near, it seemed obvious to me what could happen. In fact, I bought a small piece of adjacent swamp for $7,000 and heard the guy I bought it from laughed his butt off at how stupid I was when I bought land that couldn't be built on. Well, here is what's there now. I bought the land at an average of $30,000 an acre with a great 1930s cabin on it and sold, even the swampland, for $150,000 an acre. If you are good at seeing trends before they are popular…you know what I mean: buy low, sell high.

Since I was laid off from teaching, I started training at a national securities firm, and this was my segue into starting my financial planning practice and company. I worked my little butt off. It's risky to go from a paycheck to "no money coming in unless I get a client"…especially with 5 kids and a wife who believed in being a mother and home with her children. But after three years of hard work I left, started my own company with some partners, and in three years grew it nationwide to 14 offices and 102 representatives. In addition I was also building my own private practice.

I made an important decision at this point in my life: build a financial "empire" or coach my kids in sports? You know what I decided: to make less money, but to be independent, in control of my time, rather than dependent. So, take note: a big job with a lot of bucks doesn't necessarily make you *rich*. Once again, it's what you *do* with the money. On the right in the victory picture at a national tournament is my co-coach, Bill Schroedl, whom I mentioned earlier as a "lucky" little boomer. In front of him making the goofy face is Adriann, who has her mother's sense of humor, and second from the right, kneeling, is Erin (the twins, in other words). That is yours truly, of course, standing…yes, I am standing…on the far left.

This is Eric and Ken, then— now the cover of our company brochure, and Eric and Ken, with me in front of our Deephaven, Minnesota office. So, rather than the stress and travel involved with managing 100 represen- tatives nationwide, I simpli- fied and work with my son, my daughter Alex who runs the office, and two old family friends: Ken and Alexander, a son of a good friend, whom we hired right out of college.

We purchased a great Cape Cod when the I-394 property was developed. We bought it right—cheap—because it was in poor condition. But it was in a great neigh- borhood with large lots and we fixed it up. Thus it appreciated nicely.

We also bought some lakeshore "up north." Liking both lakeshore and the

never-ending trend of lakeshore appreciation, we took the equity from the old Cape Cod and bought this place on Lake Minnetonka. A message to remember about houses, since I'm sure you're all going to own one right away after reading this little tome: when you decide to sell, to move up to a better place or whatever…make sure your house is prepared to get the top dollar, even if you have to borrow some money short-term to make the proper improvements. It seems so obvious. The guy selling this house had some financial difficulties and was selling the house "as is" with some glaring, but inexpensive to get right, problems. He was asking $495,000 in 1994; we got it for $341,000 because, although a $20,000 improvement would probably have fetched him over $600,000, no one was going to pay that kind of money with the glaring but basically cosmetic problems with

the house. We improved the house, mostly by making it look more like a cabin (it was on a lake…even if it was upscale Lake Minnetonka) and sold it for about $1 million. As they say: they aren't making any more lakeshore.

Tim and Mary's Retirement! Well, I actually started my retirement at age 38 when I started coaching Ade and Erin's soccer team, because work became secondary to coaching. I guess you could say I saw a private practice as my transition from my "Work Days" to my "Heydays." But true independence arrived when I bought my first place, here on Lake Vermilion near the Boundary Waters, because I took the good part of a year and hid out much of the time in a room above my

wet boathouse and wrote my first novel, *A Little Short*. Since I had taught other people to write and become published authors, I wanted to try to disprove the adage: "If you can't do, teach." Then, I bought my new home on Lake Vermilion, the first piece of property I ever bought that I planned on never selling.

Okay, while it may sound like I am bragging, I feel I'm rich and I wanted to show you how I arrived at my concept of what being rich is: family, friends, health, and independence. I am what I guess people are referring to as one of the few "lucky little boomers." Also, I feel it's important you know I practice what I preach, unlike some of the more popular financial pundits. I am doing exactly what I want to be doing; and I'm in control of how I spend my time.

Questions

1. What value did you gain from my description of how "I did it"?

_____

_____

_____

_____

_____

_____

2. Has your definition of "rich" changed?
What does it now mean to you?

_____

_____

_____

_____

_____

_____

WRAP-UP

School Days

I hope you've enjoyed learning, and that your education has or will prepare you for your "Work Days." If you go directly into the work force after high school, the statistics say you'll have a rougher road to success. But many of the wealthiest clients I work with went right to a job after high school and now own their own businesses. Maybe it's street smart versus book smart, but it's mostly determination, discipline, and hard work. This could be success in the trades, or, for example, my first partner in business who dropped out of college but, through self-education, became one of the brightest minds in estate planning.

As you know by now, I am concerned about entitlement: expecting things you haven't earned. Colleges and universities have a rather unique concern about students' social progress, ego, and developing maturity due to "helicopter parents" as described in a recent *Wall Street Journal* article (7-19-08). I know this may be created by a sense of love, but it's totally bizarre to me and my wife. We saw our job as parents to raise our children to be independent, competent, and self-sufficient. I'm not going anywhere near why this "hovering" phenomenon exists, except to point out that a danger is entitlement and dependence…definite deterrents to financial independence.

Work Days

Your first job or career will probably not be your last one…but be sure to do your best, leading you to what you were meant to be. I hope your work is a passion…but keep your priorities straight. Money can provide you with independence regardless of how much you make…but family, friends, and health come first.

If you're already in the work force and in the trap of consumerism—living beyond your means, too much debt, abusing plastic—you need to participate in this revolution and change your habits…before it's too late. Time is still on your side.

Those of you preparing for new careers will be leading the revolution. Start out right…right away. The world, indeed, needs you to do this. Strange to think, but the financial debacle of 2007-2008 expanded to the entire world. It was remarkable how far-reaching the excesses of the U.S. were. Each of you changing can change the world. A little dramatic, maybe, but what do you think: the universal consumer consuming responsibly? A good idea?

Heydays

To get there earlier than the other 80%:

Live within your means...which means you:

1. Put at least 10% of your income directly into your company's retirement plan or add to an IRA on your own.

    - If there is a Roth option, invest at least 10% of your pay, being sure you're getting any matching contribution from the company.

    - If there's no Roth option, do the minimum to get the maximize match then

        - do the rest to your individual Roth IRA

        - then go back and maximize the company plan if you are able.

    - If there's no plan at work you (and your spouse whether working or not) do the max. to a Roth.

    - Establish a SEP if you're self-employed.

2. Build and maintain a cash reserve account at the bank or credit union.

    - When at a comfortable figure, start a bank draft of at least $50 a month to a mutual fund money market.

    - Work towards adding to intermediate and long-term funds in addition to the money market as soon as possible. Use a no-load like Vanguard or Fidelity, or pick a financial planner you're comfortable with, after interviewing a few.

3. Take care of your risk management.
   - Only term life insurance to begin with and only when someone is dependent on you for income.
   - Hopefully health insurance is provided. If not, get it.
   - Disability insurance, if not provided or if you're self-employed.

4. Purchase a home, with a payment within your means, as soon as you can. "Within your means" means you don't stop adding to your retirement account or cash reserve or taking care of risk management.

5. Start an education account as soon as you have a child, if only $50 a month.

6. Now you can live on the rest. Remember: **ZERO BALANCE** on credit cards. If you can't pay off your credit card balance each month, you're living beyond your means.
   - If you do this, you'll be in the 20% that will be able to do what you want to do with your life much sooner than the 80% (if they are ever able), and you can do it for as long as you choose. You'll have "bought" and earned independence.

As always, things are easier said than done…but if done, your life will be more fun and fulfilling. I hope all of you who read this will be in the 20%.

Questions

1. Do you believe you have the motivation now, or when you get your first job, to do what it takes to be in the independent 20%? Why or why not?

_____

_____

_____

_____

2. Do you think doing what I've shown you will lead to a happier, more contented, and more fulfilling life? How?

_____

_____

_____

3. They say a plan is not a plan until it's written down. Please, for your sake, write down however much in detail your behavior style allows:

_____

_____

_____

   a. What are you going to do regarding "independence" in the next month?

_____

_____

_____

b. Next year?

_____

_____

_____

c. In the next four years?

_____

_____

_____

d. Ten years from now, what should your "independence plan" look like?

_____

_____

_____

e. Just prior to "retirement," what should you be doing to be living the way you want in your Heydays? To be in control of your time...your life?

_____

_____

_____

f. What's the timeline/plan for your Heydays?

_____

_____

_____

Go ahead. Start the revolution without me. Change the world.

I'll be watching.

ENDNOTES

† *Take My Advice: Letters to the Next Generation From People Who Know a Thing or Two.* James Harmon

‡ *The 2,548 Best Things Anyone Ever Said.* Chosen and arranged by Robert Byrne.

Here is a picture of our staff at our Deephaven, MN office.

Because you showed promise as a young revolutionary by purchasing *If I Had a Million Dollars,* you'll have access to our website, **www.munkebyfinancial.com**, where I post changes and updates to the information you received. Laws change and the economy evolves, so I feel it's necessary to keep you informed.

Also, I continually add resources to help in your planning, such as balance sheets, budgeting aids and calculators where you can forecast using account values and additions at various rates of return to specified ages and income available at those time slots in your life.

I plan a sequel called *When I Have a Million Dollars,* which I would hope will continue to help you toward fulfillment and Mazlow's top level of Self-Actualization... as well as those investors in the top 20%, where, I hope, at least 80% of you will alight.

Hopefully the financial aids and updates on the website will help you all get to where you belong: Rich and Independent.

ABOUT THE AUTHOR

Tim graduated from the University of Minnesota with several degrees. He first taught English, Improvisational Theater and Creative Writing as well as coaching sports, winning two national tournaments in soccer. He then started a Financial Planning career, becoming a principal in a nationwide investment firm. He currently is Chairman of Munkeby Financial, Inc. and has been speaking to students for several years about financial independence and how that leads to a more fulfilling life. He writes both fiction and non-fiction.

Tim and his wife, Mary have been married for 43 years. They have five children and seven grandchildren—so far.

Tim and Mary now live at Lake Vermilion near the Boundary Waters. When he's not writing, reading, or speaking to young adults about Financial Literacy, he's outside on the water or in the woods.

Tim is uniquely qualified to write a readable and understandable book on a complex topic due to his successful careers in teaching young adults and building a respected financial consulting company acknowledged as a 5* Wealth Manager, the top ranking.

He hopes reading this book will have a positive impact on your life.

Visit Tim's website at: **www.timmunkeby.com**